From
PLANT
TO
PLATE

Darryl GADZEKPO & Ella PHILLIPS

Authors Darryl Gadzekpo and Ella Phillips
Illustrator Alan Berry Rhys

Senior Editor Carrie Love
Project Editor Clare Lloyd
Editor Rea Pikula
Senior Art Editor Charlotte Bull
Designer and Jacket Designer Brandie Tully-Scott
US Senior Editor Shannon Beatty
US Editor Margaret Parrish
Additional Editorial Catherine Saunders and Becca Arlington
Additional Illustration Vivian Mineker
Home Economist Denise Smart
UK Gardening Consultant Phillip Clayton
US Gardening Consultant John Tullock
Nutritionist Lucy Upton
US Culinary Consultant Renee Wilmeth
Photographer Ruth Jenkinson
Jacket Coordinator Elin Woosnam
Managing Editor Penny Smith
Managing Art Editor Diane Peyton-Jones
Senior Production Editor Nikoleta Parasaki
Senior Production Controller Inderjit Bhullar
Deputy Art Director Mabel Chan
Publisher Francesca Young
Publishing Director Sarah Larter

First American Edition, 2024
Published in the United States by DK Publishing,
a division of Penguin Random House LLC
1745 Broadway, 20th Floor, New York, NY 10019

Text copyright © Ella Phillips and
Darryl Gadzekpo 2024
Illustrations, layout and design copyright © 2024
Dorling Kindersley Limited
A Penguin Random House Company
24 25 26 27 28 10 9 8 7 6 5 4 3 2 1
001–336722–May/2024

A catalog record for this book
is available from the Library of Congress.
ISBN: 978-0-7440-9699-6

DK books are available at special discounts
when purchased in bulk for sales promotions, premiums,
fund-raising, or educational use. For details, contact:
DK Publishing Special Markets, 1745 Broadway,
20th Floor, New York, NY 10019
SpecialSales@dk.com

The recipes in this book have been created for the
ingredients and techniques indicated. The Publisher is not
responsible for your specific health or allergy needs that
may require supervision. Nor is the Publisher responsible
for any adverse reactions you may have to the recipes
contained in the book, whether you follow them as written or
modify them to suit your personal dietary needs or tastes.

Printed and bound in China

www.dk.com

This book was made with Forest
Stewardship Council™ certified
paper – one small step in DK's
commitment to a sustainable future.
Learn more at
www.dk.com/uk/information/sustainability

CONTENTS

Note from THE AUTHORS

This book is a guide to understanding our connection to food and the planet. Raising our little ones has shown us the value of learning where food comes from, and we would like to share that with you. The journey of food, be it from seed to sandwich, shovel to spoon, or plant to plate, is a magical one, and we hope this book sparks your interest to learn, eat, and grow.

You can usually find our family at our community garden or in the kitchen. We love growing what we eat, but this passion did not start with us. We've seen the joy growing plants has brought our parents and grandparents. Food brings us together. Nothing is more exciting than being able to cook what you grow and have it taste amazing! That's our kind of magic.

In this book, we will introduce you to the "earth engine," and show you how to feed your soil. No matter what size space you have, it could be as small as a boot or as big as a backyard, you can transform your seed experiments into delicious plant-powered meals!

We look at the similarities between how we care for our tummies and how we look after the earth. Join the Bug Squad as they guide you through the hidden "galaxies" below the ground and teach you how to create healthy soil. Then move above ground to learn how to grow and harvest our hero ingredients.

We are delighted to share some of our family recipes that we cook together at home. We'll show you how to turn your homegrown ingredients into delicious, plant-powered meals. So, let's begin our journey from plant to plate!

ELLA PHILLIPS   **DARRYL GADZEKPO**

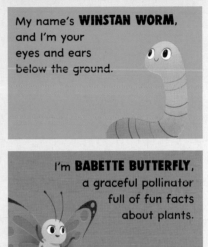

Gardening RULES

Whether you're growing fruits or vegetables in a small pot or a big garden, there are some important safety tips and rules to follow. You will need an adult with you to help with the growing activities in this book.

HYGIENE AND SAFETY

Wear old clothes, because you'll be getting your hands and your clothes dirty! You'll also need sturdy boots or shoes that you don't mind getting dirty.

Be careful around bees, wasps, and other insects. Check for them on a plant before you start weeding or watering.

If you use a wheelbarrow, ask an adult to move it for you. Wheelbarrows can be too heavy for you to handle, especially when loaded with soil.

Tie back long hair, so it doesn't get in your way or become covered in dirt.

Check with an adult before you pick and eat any fruit, mushroom, flower, or plant.

Ask an adult for help when using pruners. Pruners are incredibly sharp, so that they can cut through the stems of plants.

Some community gardens have ponds or open rain barrels. An adult should always be with you when you are near an open source of water, even if you're a very good swimmer.

Wash your hands after touching soil, compost, manure, or plants.

Wear a sun hat, apply sun screen regularly, and stay hydrated when you are outdoors, especially in warm weather.

Be careful when handling anything sharp, such as scissors. Ask an adult for help when using scissors to cut things, such as string.

Do not put your fingers or hands in your mouth if you've been working with soil, compost, or manure. They can contain harmful bacteria.

Be careful around any sharp or pointed edges, especially on recycled items that might have been cut or repurposed.

Depending on where you live in the world, certain animals might visit your growing location! Do not touch them and alert an adult if you see any dangerous animals.

Cover the tops of growing stakes with small plastic bottles, so that there is no chance of accidentally poking yourself on them.

Do not touch any garden chemicals. We don't use any chemicals (pesticides) in this book, but you might still come across them, especially if you're planting in a community garden or shared space.

Be careful when using a hand fork or a rake, as they have sharp points.

Kitchen RULES

Being in the kitchen is so much fun, but there are plenty of potential hazards, too. Follow these steps so you don't hurt yourself. **You will need an adult to help you with all of the recipes in this book.**

When you see the warning triangle, take extra care and ask an adult for help.

KITCHEN SAFETY

Be careful around hot ovens and gas or electric stovetops. Make sure you know when the oven or stovetop is on, and wear oven mitts if you touch anything that might be hot. Let an adult move baking sheets and pans in and out of the oven.

There are some steps in the recipes that an adult must complete. Do not try to do them yourself. If in doubt, ask an adult to help with any part of the recipe.

Get an adult to help with any hot liquids and hot pans. Always protect your hands with oven mitts when moving or holding hot items. Tell an adult immediately if you get a burn.

Ask an adult for help with electrical appliances, such as a blender. Always turn appliances off at the socket when they are not in use. Never put your hands near the moving parts.

Be careful when using sharp items, such as knives, a grater, or a peeler. Take extra care and ask an adult to help when cutting a fruit or vegetable that has thick skin, such as a butternut squash. You can also wear cut-resistant gloves to protect your hands.

Before getting started, roll up your sleeves, tie back long hair, and put on an apron.

Kitchen hygiene

When you're in the kitchen, you need to follow these important rules to keep germs in check.
- Always wash your hands before you start any recipe.
- Keep your cooking area clean and use hot, soapy water to clean cutting boards after each use.
- Wash all fruits and vegetables before using.
- Check the use-by date on all ingredients. Consider that "best before" is not the same as "use by."

Ingredients and equipment

- Assemble all your ingredients and equipment before you start to make a recipe. You'll probably have most ingredients in your kitchen already, but you might need to buy some. You may need to borrow some of the equipment, or buy it new.
- Always use the type of flour specified in a recipe.
- Follow the temperature instructions for preheating the oven found within each recipe.

WEIGHTS AND MEASUREMENTS

Carefully measure the ingredients before you start a recipe. Use measuring spoons, weighing scales, or a measuring cup, as necessary. Below are the abbreviations for the measurements used in this book.

METRIC
g = gram
kg = kilogram
ml = milliliter
cm = centimeter

US STANDARD
oz = ounce
lb = pound
fl oz = fluid ounce
in = inch

SPOON MEASURES
tsp = teaspoon
tbsp = tablespoon

BE ALLERGY AWARE!

Always check that the ingredients for a recipe do not contain anything that you, or a friend, or anyone eating the meals might be allergic to or that is not otherwise part of your recommended diet.

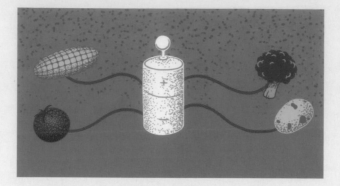

POWER UP

Let's explore what your body needs to stay strong and healthy. Discover how to tap into your inner superhero using the magic of plants.

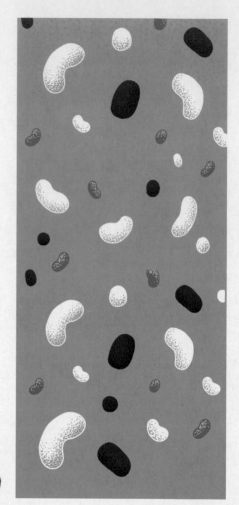

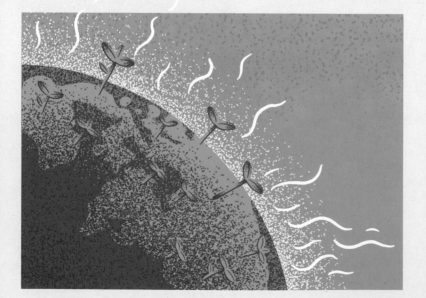

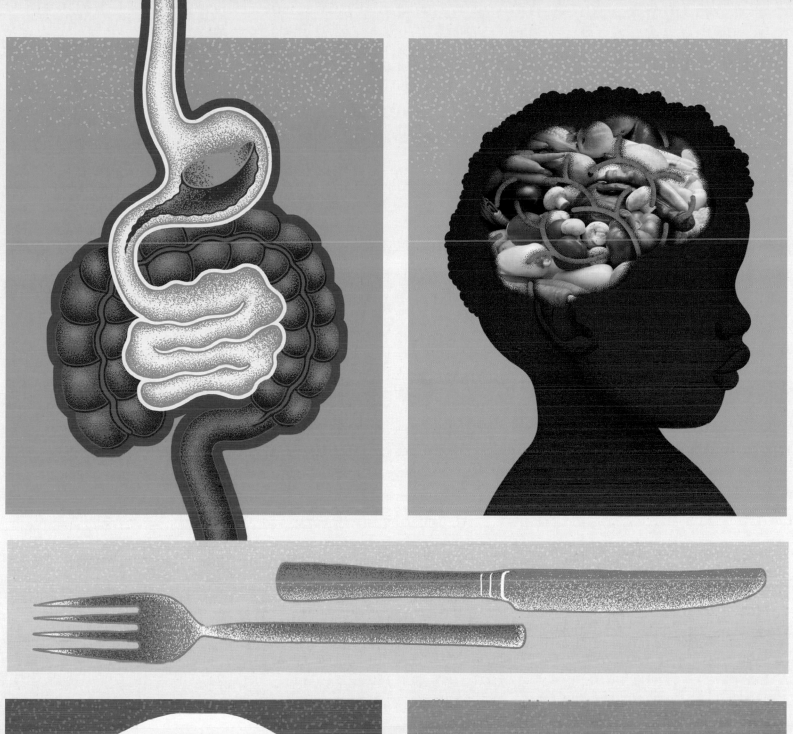

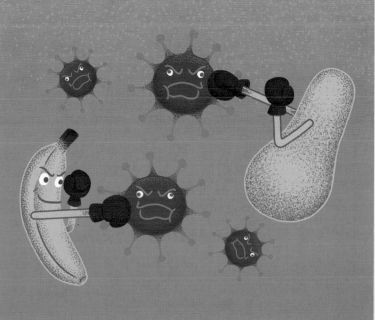

Get to know DIGESTION

When you eat, different parts of your body, from your mouth to your bottom, work to break down food into nutrients. This is called digestion. Think of the digestive system as an engine that releases and sends out energy around the body so it can function properly.

Mouth

As you chew, your teeth break food down into smaller pieces. Saliva mixes with the food and breaks it down even further, so it's swallowed more easily.

Esophagus

From your mouth, food makes its way down a tube called the esophagus to your stomach.

Stomach

With the help of some strong muscles and an acid called gastric juice, your stomach churns and mashes food until it turns into a mushy liquid.

Small intestine

This liquid travels into your small intestine and is broken down into tiny chemicals. These chemicals pass into your blood through the walls of the small intestine and are carried around your body.

❺ Large intestine

Food that cannot be digested passes into your large intestine. This waste is then kept in a storage site near your bottom, called the rectum, until you go to the bathroom.

If you chew your food well, it makes it easier for your body to digest it. So, take your time. Slow and steady wins the race.

Inside the GUT

Your gut, which is the stomach, small intestine, and large intestine, is at the heart of digestion.

Microscopic microbes

There are trillions of tiny living creatures called microbes in your gut. The majority of these microbes are bacteria. These tiny guests help you get nutrients from your food. They also boost your immune system, which is the network of cells, tissues, and organs in your body that fight off illness.

Your body consists of around 30 trillion human cells and roughly 40 trillion bacteria cells.

Did you know that all of the microbes in your body together weigh about the same as your brain?

The bacteria in your gut love fiber. Give them the fiber in fruits and veggies, and, in return, they will help with digestion.

BACTERIA BREAKDOWN

A healthy gut wastes nothing. Fiber that can't be absorbed by your body is broken down by the bacteria in your large intestine. This helps to unlock vital vitamins that your body can't make on its own.

Microbes are so tiny that you can only see them if you view them under a microscope.

FOOD *is* FUEL

Just as biodiversity helps the Earth to thrive, a diverse diet helps your body to stay healthy. Your job is to make sure you get the right amounts of different foods so you eat a well-balanced diet. Keep your tummy and taste buds happy by eating a mix of foods.

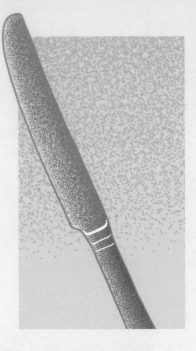

VEGETABLES

Vegetables, which include herbs, create a healthy, fiber-packed environment for the bacteria in your gut. A happy tummy leads to a happy body!

Try to eat 20 different types of fruits, vegetables, herbs, and spices every week.

FRUITS

Apples, berries, pears, and other fruits provide your body with much-needed vitamins, while giving you a boost of sugar. Replace refined sugar-packed snacks with fresh, natural alternatives made with fruit.

TOP TIP!

Eat fruits, such as dates, as a sweet treat. They contain lots of fiber, so they will fill you up.

FATS AND OILS

Olive oil, coconut oil, and seeds will keep you working like a well-oiled machine. These healthy fats help improve the movement of electrical signals (communication) between body parts.

LEGUMES

Beans and peas are legumes, which are great sources of protein. Proteins are the building blocks of your body, and each one contains different combinations of amino acids. Your body needs these to grow and repair, so make sure to eat a variety of proteins.

GRAINS

Brown rice, millet, and amaranth contain carbohydrates and are amazing slow-release energy sources. Add them to your meals so you feel full and energized!

WATER

All living things need water. In fact, water makes up 50 percent of a human's body. Try to drink 6-8 glasses of water a day to help your body perform all of its tasks.

VITAMIN	WHAT YOU USE IT FOR	GOOD SOURCES	
Vitamin A (retinols and carotenoids)	Eye health, helps the immune system	Fruits and vegetables, especially orange varieties	
Vitamin B1 (thiamine)	Breaking down carbohydrates, muscle contraction	Whole grains, lentils, beans, peas	
Vitamin B2 (riboflavin)	Enzyme function, breaking down fats, proteins, and carbohydrates	Green vegetables, quinoa, mushrooms, almonds	
Vitamin B3 (niacin)	Cell and nerve function, releasing energy from food, metabolism	Grains, sunflower seeds, fortified breakfast cereals, peanuts	
Vitamin B5 (pantothenic acid)	Breaking down fats and carbohydrates, production of red blood cells	Fortified breakfast cereals, dried mushrooms, sunflower seeds, avocados	
Vitamin B6 (pyridoxine)	Helps the immune system	Legumes, oats, fruits and vegetables, especially bananas	
Vitamin B7 (biotin)	Bone and hair health	Whole wheat bread, peanuts, green leafy vegetables	
Vitamin B9 (folic acid or folate)	Production of red blood cells, cell function	Green vegetables, beans, lentils	
Vitamin B12 (cobalamin)	Production of red blood cells, nerve function	Fortified breakfast cereals	
Vitamin C (ascorbic acid)	Cell function, helps the immune system	Fruits and vegetables, fruit juices	
Vitamin D (calciferol)	Bone health	Mushrooms, fortified plant-based milk alternatives, sunlight	
Vitamin E (tocopherols and tocotrienols)	Cell function, helps the immune system	Sunflower oil, nuts, seeds, whole grains	
Vitamin K	Enzyme function	Green leafy vegetables, kiwi fruits, cashew nuts	

> Plants that are grown in nutrient-rich soil with plenty of sunshine and water will contain lots of vitamins and minerals.

> Your body needs 13 essential vitamins and 16 essential minerals.

VITAMINS and MINERALS

Vitamins and minerals are like superheroes. They have different roles, but they work together to ensure your body stays strong and healthy. Vitamins help you function properly. Minerals help your body grow and repair itself.

Valuable vitamins

Most of the vitamins you need to survive are made by plants and animals, so you need to consume the vitamins in food or drink. You can make a few on your own, such as vitamins D and K.

MINERAL	WHAT YOU USE IT FOR	GOOD SOURCES	
Calcium	Bone and teeth health, muscle contraction	Fortified plant-based milk alternatives, green leafy vegetables	
Phosphorus	Bone and cell health	Nuts, lentils, kidney beans, cashew nuts	
Magnesium	Bone and tissues health, enzymes, muscles, and nerve health	Pumpkin seeds, quinoa, green leafy vegetables, nuts	
Sodium	Body water levels, electrolyte balance	Salty foods (seaweed, pickles, olives)	
Potassium	Cell and nerve function, electrolyte and water balance	Beans, potatoes, dried fruits, bananas, butternut squash	
Sulfur	Muscle health, cell repair, and enzyme health	Nuts, seeds, grains, lentils	
Iron	Transporting oxygen around the body, blood production, and helping the immune system	Pulses, fortified breakfast cereals, pumpkin seeds, leafy vegetables, dried figs, apricots	
Fluoride	Bone and teeth health	Fluorinated tap water, raisins, grapes	
Chlorine	Production of stomach acids, cell function	Sea salt, seaweed	
Copper	Enzyme function	Nuts, seeds, whole grains	
Zinc	Enzyme function	Legumes, nuts, oatmeal	
Manganese	Enzyme function	Grains, seeds, nuts, green vegetables	
Molybdenum	Breaking down proteins	Legumes, nuts, bananas, grains	
Iodine	Hormone production	Seaweed (but eat in moderation, as it's high in salt)	
Chromium	Breaking down sugars and fats	Broccoli, grape juice, potatoes, whole grains	
Selenium	Enzyme function	Brazil nuts, seeds, grains, mushrooms, asparagus	

Magical minerals

Minerals are found in rocks and soil, but you can't eat either of those! Luckily, bacteria in the soil breaks down the minerals so plants can absorb them. Then you eat the plants to get the minerals.

Dynamic duos

Some vitamins and minerals are stronger together than apart. Vitamin D and calcium work as a team to get your muscles moving. Zinc carries vitamin A to your eyes to keep them healthy and bright.

The word "vitamin" was created in 1912 by a biochemist named Casimir Funk.

How to FEED YOUR BODY'S NEEDS

Now you know what your body needs, let's find out how to get it. Start by "eating the rainbow." Regularly eating a range of colored foods gives your body the best chance of getting all the nutrients it needs to stay healthy. Here are a few examples of how different colored foods help your body.

Balanced bacteria

If you've eaten a tasty array of colorful, fiber-packed fruits and veggies, the bacteria in your gut will be happy. That's because they love to feed on fiber. When the bacteria are happy and balanced, they help your body absorb the nutrients it needs to function as it should.

RED

Red foods are usually packed with vitamin C. Fruits and vegetables such as red bell peppers, tomatoes, watermelon, and strawberries have powerful antioxidants, which keep your heart and blood healthy.

ORANGE AND YELLOW

Orange and yellow foods are high in vitamin C and carotenoids, which work wonders for your immune system and promote healthy skin and eyes.

Color matching

Mixing colors together on your plate is an easy way to make your meal look great and to pack it with combinations that boost health. Here are some suggestions and how they benefit your body.

GREEN

Green vegetables are great for your digestion and eyesight, due to their richness in fiber and lutein (known as the "eye vitamin").

BLUE AND PURPLE

Blue and purple fruits and vegetables are high in antioxidants. They're like superhero helpers that keep tiny troublemakers in your body, called free radicals, from causing too much damage.

WHITE AND BROWN

White and brown foods are where you find proteins that help you to grow, as well as carbohydrates, which are your body's main energy source.

⬤ + ⬤ = **SUPER VISION**

⬤ + ⬤ = **BUILDING BONES**

⬤ + ⬤ + ⬤ = **MUSCLE POWER**

⬤ + ⬤ + ⬤ = **HEALTHY IMMUNE SYSTEM**

Dig into a delicious rice dish with red bell peppers, orange squash, yellow zucchini, and green leaves. Then finish it off with ice cream topped with blueberries, indigo plums, and scattered violets. Now that's rainbow plant-power!

Plant-powered EATING

Plants power your body from the inside out. By eating them every day—whether that's on their own or as part of recipes, you benefit from their useful deliciousness! They contain vitamins, minerals, water, and fiber—all things your body needs to stay healthy and perform at its best. From super vision to super strength, plant-power keeps you flying high!

What is plant-powered eating?

Plant-powered eating means fueling your body with a range of plants, such as fruits, veggies, grains, and legumes. Your body is like a battery that needs plants to charge it up, so your bones and muscles can grow strong and your gut can stay healthy.

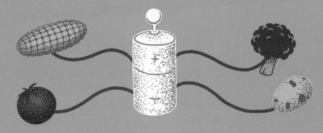

What do you eat?

For ultimate plant-power and healthy living, we "eat the rainbow." This means making sure the fruits and vegetables on your plate are as colorful and varied as possible.

What would you have on your plate? There are lots of different ideas in this book, so get ready to find some new favorites!

Fighting disease

Plant-powered eating does a great job of supporting your immune system, which keeps you healthy and protects you from infections, such as the flu. This is why adults tell you to eat lots of fruits and vegetables when you're feeling under the weather!

Eating plants helps the planet

Plants absorb carbon dioxide and produce oxygen that humans and animals need to survive. When more plants are grown for people to eat, this means there is more oxygen available for humans to breathe.

BEANS ARE PLANTS, TOO!

Beans are packed full of important amino acids. Think of your body as a construction site. Amino acids are the bricks and mortar that help build and repair everything from your bones to your skin. And just as a builder needs good materials to work with, your body needs a steady supply of amino acids to keep growing and repairing itself.

Some of the strongest animals are plant-powered, from the enormous elephant to the giant gorilla!

I'm plant-powered! I eat plant scraps to create energy for myself and poop out something called a casting, which contains nutrients for the soil.

An animal that only eats plants is called a herbivore.

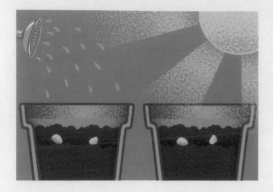

PLANT

Get ready to explore the amazing world of planting! We're here to show you how to grow cool plants and to share our fun gardening tricks. Let's discover secrets from underground to above, and keep your plants super happy!

GARDENING *tools*

To grow the fruits, vegetables, and herbs in this book, you'll need these pieces of equipment.

HERO RECIPE

Basil pesto pasta

This icon tells you which recipe in the book uses the food you've grown as its main ingredient.

Seed tray

Plastic wrap

String

Soil

Seeds

Seed packet

Gravel, sand, and small stones

Pruners

Potting mix

Seed starting mix

Spade

Trowel

Bucket

Watering can

Rake

Compost bin

Gardening gloves

Soft fruit tray

Shovel

Bamboo stakes

Mulch

Assortment of pots

Follow the instructions on these icons as you grow the plants.

PLANTING SEASON

This symbol tells you the best time of year to start planting.

SOIL TYPE

All of the plants in this book can be grown directly in the ground or in an assortment of pots. If you choose to grow the plants in the ground, this symbol tells you the best soil for each plant.

AMOUNT OF LIGHT

Look for this symbol—it tells you how much light each plant needs.

From SEED TO plant

Plants are living things that can grow just about anywhere. They are so much more than they seem. Without them, we wouldn't have oxygen to breathe.

What is a seed?

A seed is a special package that has a baby plant inside and everything it needs to grow. Seeds can be as tiny as a speck of dust or as big as a beach ball. With the right environment, seeds can grow into healthy plants that produce even more seeds.

What is a bulb?

Bulbs are plants with special swollen leaves that store water and nutrients (food) to help the plant survive cold or dry conditions. When conditions are right, bulbs begin to grow; some can form baby bulbs that become new plants without having grown from seeds.

You can eat certain bulbs, such as onions and garlic. You can eat some seeds, too, such as sunflower and pumpkin seeds.

Seeds are like cocoons, but for plants! The biggest seed in the world is the sea coconut from the Seychelles islands in Africa; it can grow up to 20in (50cm) wide.

Sea coconut seed

Coconut

Where to get your seeds

A magical way to get seeds is from the plants, fruits, and vegetables that you have grown. In most plants, there are enough seeds to grow hundreds more plants. To save seeds, separate your seeds from the plant and store them in a cool dry place. Beans can dry on their stems.

Some fruits, such as avocados, have stones or pits, which contain the seeds. You can grow new plants from these, too.

How to sow seds

When you have chosen your seeds, you need to know how to sow them. Some seeds can simply be scattered across the top of the soil. Others need to be buried in the soil, which means getting out your trowel or shovel and digging.

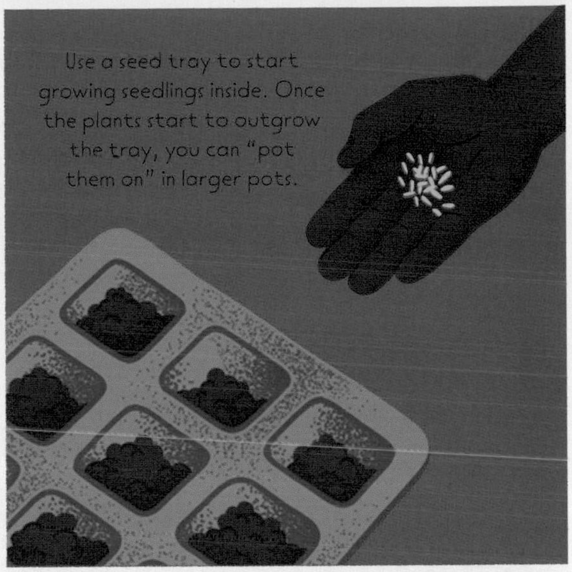

Some seeds need to be covered with soil in order to grow.

Use a seed tray to start growing seedlings inside. Once the plants start to outgrow the tray, you can "pot them on" in larger pots.

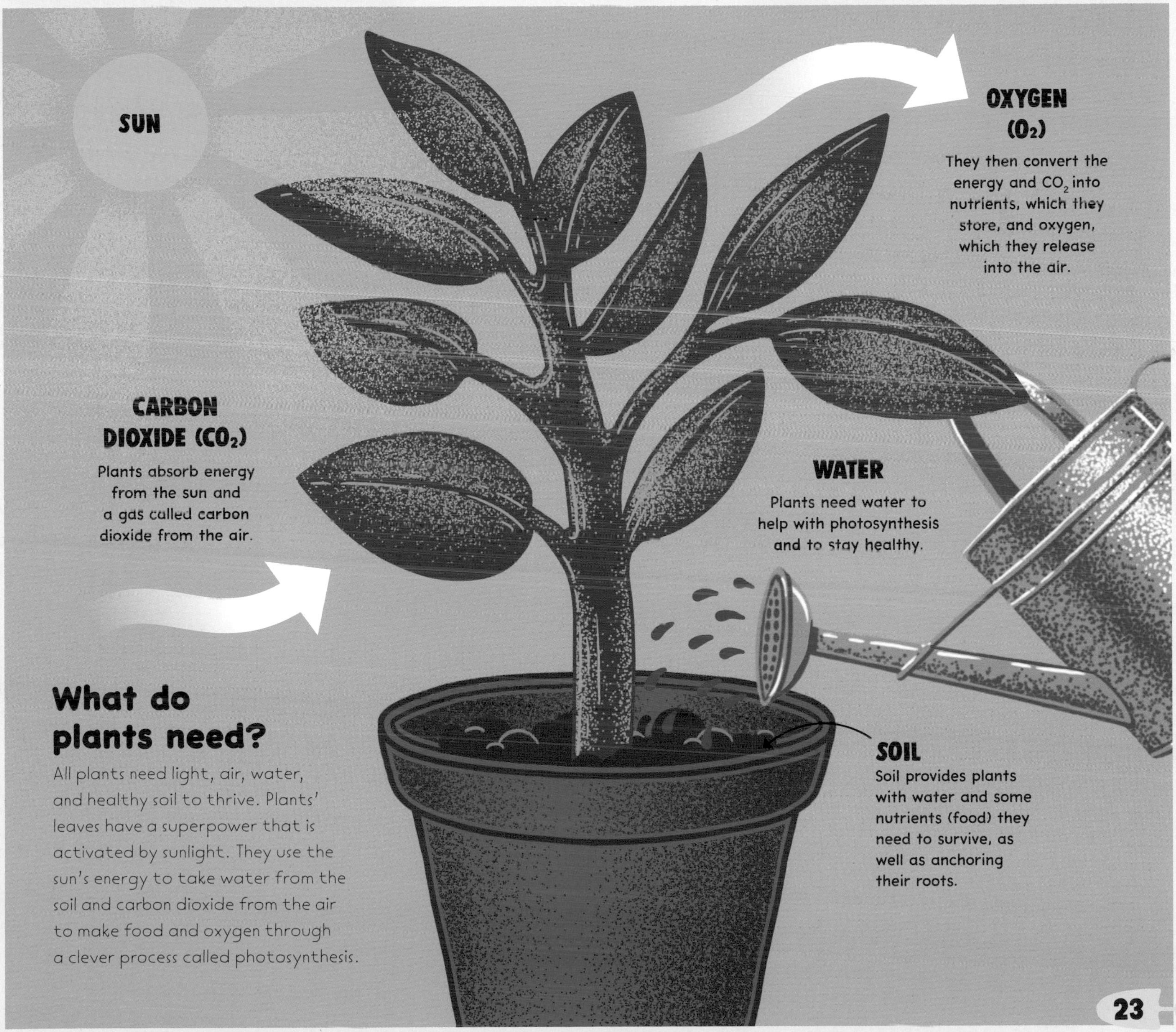

SUN

OXYGEN (O_2)

They then convert the energy and CO_2 into nutrients, which they store, and oxygen, which they release into the air.

CARBON DIOXIDE (CO_2)

Plants absorb energy from the sun and a gas called carbon dioxide from the air.

WATER

Plants need water to help with photosynthesis and to stay healthy.

What do plants need?

All plants need light, air, water, and healthy soil to thrive. Plants' leaves have a superpower that is activated by sunlight. They use the sun's energy to take water from the soil and carbon dioxide from the air to make food and oxygen through a clever process called photosynthesis.

SOIL

Soil provides plants with water and some nutrients (food) they need to survive, as well as anchoring their roots.

BENEATH the GROUND

Below your feet is a whole "galaxy" waiting to be discovered, where microscopic organisms, burrowing and wriggling animals, and creepy-crawlies live. Each one plays a role in keeping the soil balanced and your plants well-fed.

Bacteria in the soil help plants absorb food, just like the ones in your tummy do.

Plant ROOTS

As they reach down into the soil, roots hold plants in place. They also suck up water and nutrients (food) from the soil. But often they need help getting all of that food.

Sugars move down the sugar "highways."

PLANT PARTNERS

Some plants are good friends with fungi and bacteria. They'll send down sugars, and, in return, the fungi and bacteria provide the roots with food that they can't reach on their own.

SUGAR STREETS

Plants have sugar "highways" that run through the stems and roots. Sugars that plants have produced during photosynthesis travel along these highways. Nutrients jump onto the "highways", then travel up the roots and stems to the rest of the plant.

Nutrients go up the "highways."

RECYCLERS

Plant roots can't eat the dead plants and animals in the soil, but wriggling worms can. Their poop contains nutrients that the plants can eat.

All about SOIL

Getting to know your soil is the first
step to happy planting.

Soil pH

The pH scale is used to measure how acidic or alkaline a
liquid is. Acids have a pH that is lower than 7, and alkalis
have a pH that is higher than 7. Most plants can only
thrive in soil that has a pH level of between 5.5 and 7.5.
Anything more or less, and your plants won't be
able to soak up the nutrients they need.

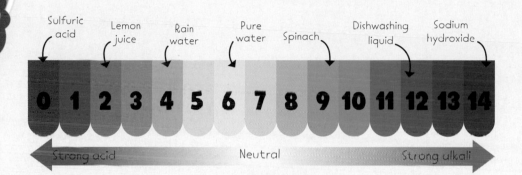

Sulfuric acid — Lemon juice — Rain water — Pure water — Spinach — Dishwashing liquid — Sodium hydroxide

0 1 2 3 4 5 6 7 8 9 10 11 12 13 14

Strong acid — Neutral — Strong alkali

CHAIN REACTION

Bacteria and fungi produce
chemicals, called enzymes,
which break down dead
plants and animals into
food that plants
can absorb.

Sorting soil

All soil is made up of air, water, dead plants and animals, and
broken down rock (minerals). But there are different types of soil,
such as sand, silt, clay, and loam. Your soil type will impact how
well your soil holds water, how nutrient-rich it is,
and how well it drains water.

The best way to know which soil you have is to collect a handful
of soil and roll it into a ball. Pure silt soil is typically found around
rivers, so you are unlikely to have this in your garden.

The best soil for most
plants is loam, which is
40% sand, 40% silt,
and 20% clay.

Clay soil will keep its
shape without crumbling.

If the soil molds into a ball
fairly well, then it's loam.

If the soil falls apart,
it is sandy.

Clever COMPOSTING

Food scraps and garden waste can be broken down into a clever mixture called "compost." When compost is combined with soil, it's like rocket fuel for your plants. You need a mix of different types of waste, water, air, patience, and some expert help from the Bug Squad to ensure that the recipe for compost is perfect.

TOP TIP!

Do not put meat, dairy, and oily foods in the compost, as they can attract pests and cause bad smells.

You will need

- Compost bin
- Green waste
- Brown waste
- Rake or shovel

1

Start by placing the compost bin in a shady but warm area of your yard.

2

Green waste

Brown waste

Fill your bin with a 1½–2½in (4–6cm) layer of green waste, followed by a layer of brown waste. Alternate green and brown layers until they are 3ft (1m) high. Then leave the waste to work its magic.

3

Regularly water the compost heap. Every few weeks, turn (mix) it using the rake or shovel. This allows air to flow, which makes it easier for helpful bacteria to break down the mixture.

4

Over time, the compost heap rots and it generates heat.

5

Be patient. Compost can take 3–6 months to be ready to use. Finished compost should be rich and crumbly, but the ultimate test is the smell test. If it smells bad, it is not ready!

Mulching

This is a great way to recycle and reuse in your garden and give your plants some extra moisture. Spread a layer of your composted garden waste on the surface of the soil around a plant to help feed it and keep in moisture. You can also add wood chips, tree bark, or well-rotted manure.

Wood chips

Change IT UP!

Using a special compost bin is not the only way to start composting.

You can turn a store-bought garbage can into a compost bin. Ask an adult to drill holes along the side of the bin so your compost can get plenty of air.

Creepy-crawlies in your compost

If you look at your compost heap, you'll see lots of bugs. But what are they doing there?

> All bugs play an important role in helping your plants to grow!

> I love eating compost for dinner! I poop out the waste, which is rich in nutrients and is a natural fertilizer for plants.

> I make tunnels in the compost. This gives good bacteria air and space to break down waste.

You can simply create your compost heap in a shady corner of your yard. Place a sheet of cardboard down first.

You can get cardboard, coffee grounds, and wood chips for free from local garden centers and businesses. This reuse reduces waste and helps with biodiversity.

WHAT happens above GROUND?

Above ground, the living world is visible. Plants stretch toward the sun, insects crawl, fly, or slither, and birds sing. To understand how to grow plants, it's useful to know how they work and what you need to consider to get the best out of them.

Flowers

More than just a beautiful decoration, a flower attracts insects, birds, and other animals that help the plant make seeds. Parts of the flower also grow into fruit. The seed of a sunflower is considered a fruit.

All flowering plants produce fruit, but the fruit is not always edible!

Leaves

Leaves are packed with a magical green substance called chlorophyll. This is able to convert sunlight into food for the plant. Like leaves, your skin also uses sunlight, but in a slightly different way—it uses it to make vitamin D.

Stem

This is the tubelike part of the plant that holds the leaves and flowers. It carries water and food from the roots to all parts of the plant—just like your veins carry blood to your heart.

Weather woes

Plants need sun and water, but too much rain (or not enough) may spell the end of their life. Gentle breezes keep pests and diseases away, but strong winds can snap stems and make plants thirsty. Some plants can cope with extreme weather conditions thanks to their deep roots, waxy leaves, or hairy stems.

POLLINATOR PLANTS

Invite friendly pollinators to your garden by planting lots of bright, fragrant blooms that they can feed on. Choose plants that haven't been treated with pesticides.

Coneflower

Sunflower

Marigold

Basil

Lavender

Nature's helpers

Pollination is how plants make seeds. But plants need a helping hand from either the wind or animals such as birds, bees, wasps, and butterflies to spread their pollen around.

1 Halle Honeybee visits flowers to drink a tasty sweet liquid called nectar.

2 Pollen from the flowers stick to Halle's body. She then drops the pollen onto other flowers she visits on her adventure.

3 The pollen joins with an egg inside the flower and a seed starts to form. When these seeds drop to the ground, they start to grow into baby plants.

Protect
YOUR PLANTS

Plants have the ability to attract pollinators, they can work together in happy partnerships, and they can let you know when something is wrong. But the key to healthy plants is paying attention to them.

Problem SOLVING

You can tell a lot about how healthy plants are by looking at them. Here are some common problems that plants face, and how to fix them.

Are your plant's leaves turning slightly yellow or even crispy? Is the soil dry to the touch?

Your plant is too dry and needs to be watered.

Does your plant have floppy leaves and stems? Does the soil feel soggy?

Your plant may be too wet, so stop watering it until it's nearly dry all the way through.

Is your plant pale with small leaves and long thin stems that are reaching up to the light?

Your plant may need more sun. Move it to a brighter place where it can catch some rays.

Nature's highlighters

Who is visiting your plants? Is it friendly bugs, such as bumblebees, or pests, like aphids, which attack plants?

Scientists have found that most pests are less interested in healthy plants. When plants get weak, their bodies change and they become easier food for the nibbling nasties.

So, pests are clues that your plants or soil need help. Then you can begin your detective work and fix the problem!

Best BUDDIES

When certain plants grow close to each other, they can encourage helpful insects, keep unhelpful ones away, and make each other stronger. This is called companion planting, and it is a bit like having a best friend in the garden.

THE THREE SISTERS

This is a special way of growing corn, beans, and squash together. These three "sisters" work together to help each other grow. Teamwork makes the dream work!

The corn grows tall and helps the beans to climb.

The beans feed the corn and the squash by putting a gas called nitrogen into the soil.

The squash spreads out on the ground, keeping it moist and making it hard for weeds to grow.

Ground cover

Crops called "cover crops" can help shelter soil and plants from wind, sun, and rain. Giant goosefoot is a great example of this. It can grow up to 5ft (1.5m) high, but it's easy to remove if you need space.

Plant defenders

Marigolds can protect other plant roots with their clever chemicals and confuse predators with their scent. They also attract ladybugs and hoverflies, which eat pests.

Distraction plants
LET IT GO!

Grow plants that bugs find tasty near your favorite plants, to keep them safe from nibbling insects. You can plant nasturtiums next to beans so that aphids eat them instead.

Repelling plants
STAY AWAY!

These bold plants keep pests away with their strong smell. Plant garlic around kale and potatoes to put off aphids and whiteflies.

Space savers
ROOM FOR ALL!

Plants with roots at different soil depths don't compete for nutrients (food) and water, so you can plant them close together. This is the case with spinach and broccoli.

BIODIVERSITY

Biodiversity refers to the variety of living things in a particular area. The more diverse an area is with plant and animal life, the healthier it should be. This is because each plant and animal plays a vital role in maintaining a thriving ecosystem.

An ecosystem is like a big family of plants, animals, and other living things that all live together in one place, such as a forest, desert, or pond.

Celebrating difference

Without a wide range of animals and plants, we wouldn't have the talented team that we rely on to do things such as fight disease and create food. Differences make us stronger, and everyone needs each other to succeed!

FEEDING THE SOIL

A mixture of rotting plants and animals provides food for the soil.

NUTRIENT CYCLING

Plants and animals help to move minerals and nutrients (food) around the soil.

How does VARIETY help the SOIL?

Our shared family tree

Since the earliest times, people have grown plants together. Communities have always understood the importance of biodiversity. From the Akan of Ghana to the Caribs of Dominica, the Māori of New Zealand to the Navajo of North America, they all know that everything is connected in a shared family tree.

BIODIVERSITY BADGE

TOP TIP!

Look for this biodiversity badge! This shows the different varieties of plants, fruits, and vegetables that can be grown and eaten.

FUN FACTS!

Even tiny organisms play an important role in the health of large ecosystems.

Lichens are organisms made up of fungi and algae or bacteria. They create habitats for animals, provide nesting material for birds, and help plants get food from a gas called nitrogen. They can tell us about the environment, such as changes in climate.

Ladybirds are powerful pollinators and help to control pests. They are sensitive creatures, so they often let us know whether the ecosystem is healthy or not.

STAYING HYDRATED

The underground network created by roots helps water to move through the soil and improves soil nutrition.

SOIL HELPERS

Some plants can repel pests that may harm the soil, while others attract insects that help the soil.

Set up your EARTH ENGINE

An earth engine is the power base that every plant needs to grow. It's a place where you generate healthy soil to grow plants. It can be anything from a garden to a boot. The earth engine is where you power up your soil, so plants can take off!

WHERE TO GROW

A windowsill is the perfect spot for a small earth engine. If your plant needs to be grown in a larger container, you can place it on a doorstep or balcony or in the yard.

Space savers

Cardboard boxes, cups, cans, old shoes, and plastic bottles and boxes are examples of small earth engines.

Be careful, as the edges of cans are sharp. Ask an adult for help.

Ask an adult to cut off the tops of used plastic bottles.

Mighty mediums

Big pots, sacks, boots, and hanging baskets are great medium-sized earth engines.

Living large

If you need a bigger growing space, then use raised beds, your own garden, or a community garden.

RAISED BEDS

GARDEN

EARTH ENGINE
basics

No matter what earth engine you choose to grow your plants in, they will need the right underground home. Layer by layer, build up the strength of your soil.

 Most seeds should be sown at a depth twice their width. If the seeds are very small, water the soil before planting them, since this reduces the chance that the seeds will get washed away.

1 Make sure that your earth engine has drainage holes spaced ¾-1in (2-3cm) apart in the bottom. If not, ask an adult to drill holes. This helps water and air pass through the soil.

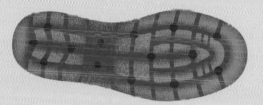

2 Add twigs and branches. These will eventually rot down and be food for worms, fungi, and bacteria.

3 Add potting mix combined with soil and worms. Your earth engine should be alive with bugs and bacteria. Then add your seeds, cover them with potting mix or soil, and top with mulch, such as leaves and rotted wood chips.

Add small stones, gravel, or sand at the bottom of your earth engine to help with drainage.

TOP TIP!

If your earth engine is indoors, place a saucer or tray underneath it to catch water runoff.

COMMUNITY GARDEN

SOIL VS. COMPOST

Soil is made up of air, water, and particles of rock mixed with the remains of dead animals and plants. Compost is made from food waste and rotting plants, and it helps to improve soil.

HERBS

Herbs play a bigger role in your daily life than you might think. These plants are used for their delightful flavors and scents, and even as a way to help keep people healthy.

HERB OR SPICE?

A herb is typically the fresh leafy part of a plant. A spice is usually dried, and it comes from a plant's seeds, buds, roots, stems, fruits, flowers, or bark.

Thyme (herb)

Cinnamon (spice)

Terrific taste

No kitchen is complete without herbs to add delicious new flavors to your meals.

Thyme

There are more than 300 varieties of thyme, but, generally, all have an earthy flavor that pairs well with roasted veggies.

Sorrel

Before lemons became widely available, sorrel was used to add a slightly sour flavor to food.

Sensational scents

Some herbs have fragrant leaves, which, in addition to smelling nice, have many practical uses.

Lavender

Its sweet and floral scent is used in perfumes, soaps, body washes, and air fresheners.

Rosemary

Its strong scent can repel flies, mosquitoes, and cabbage moths from your garden.

There are herbs all around you! Next time you are outside, follow your nose. You will soon learn to recognize herbs by their smell!

Wonderful well-being

For thousands of years, many people have believed that herbs can help you feel better.

Sage

It is packed with vitamin K, which helps wounds to heal.

Chamomile

Some people find drinking chamomile tea relaxing and calming.

Grow BASIL

Known as the "royal plant," basil is a sweet herb that is packed with valuable vitamins, such as vitamin K, for kings. In hot climates, basil grows all year round. It's best kept on a sunny windowsill or in a greenhouse.

 Plant in spring/summer

 Grow in well-drained loam soil, pH 6-7.5

Grow in a sunny place

You will need
- Small pot
- Potting mix
- Basil seeds
- Plastic wrap or clear plastic bag

 **HERO RECIPE**
Basil pesto pasta

1 Fill the small pot with potting mix, then water. Thinly scatter several basil seeds on top, then cover with a thin layer of potting mix. Place in a sunny spot and water regularly.

Potting mix
Seeds
Potting mix

2 To help keep the potting mix moist and warm, cover the pot with plastic wrap or the plastic bag. When the basil plants start to sprout, remove the cover and let them grow.

Cling film

 **HARVEST TIME!**

3 When the plants are 6in (15cm) to 8in (20cm) tall, start picking the leaves. Collect the leaves from the top branches.

8in (20cm)
6in (15cm)

BIODIVERSITY BADGE

There are so many varieties of basil. The most common type is sweet basil, but other types include rich African blue basil, tasty liquorice-like Thai basil, and lemon basil.

Sweet basil

Thai basil

Lemon basil

African blue basil

A happy home

Basil belongs to the same family of herbs as rosemary and thyme. Don't let that trick you! They don't grow well together.

Meet some of the herbs that, like basil, prefer to grow in moist soil and can join it in your garden.

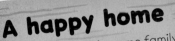

Used in Italian cooking, mostly in sauces and salads.

Sprinkle this over pizza.

Has a green onion flavor.

Has a refreshing taste and is found in chewing gum and toothpaste.

Has a peppery flavor.

Basil

Oregano

Chives

Mint

Cress

Grow CHERRY TOMATOES

The best way to get the tastiest cherry tomatoes to feast on is to grow your own. You can even save the seeds of a tomato you've really enjoyed eating and use them to grow a new crop.

I feed on pests that attack your tomato plants, such as aphids. Plant marigolds near your tomatoes to attract me!

 Plant in spring

 Grow in well-drained loam soil, pH 6-7

 Grow in a sunny place

You will need

- Seed tray
- Seed starting mix
- Tomato seeds
- Plastic wrap or clear plastic bag
- Small pots
- Potting mix
- Large pots 12in (30cm) wide
- String
- Bamboo stakes

BIODIVERSITY BADGE

Cherry tomatoes aren't always red. You can grow tasty orange, yellow, green, and black varieties.

1

Fill the seed tray with the seed starting mix. Water well. Add 3 seeds per cell and cover with a thin layer of compost. Put plastic wrap or the plastic bag over the tray and place on a warm windowsill. Water every 3-4 days.

2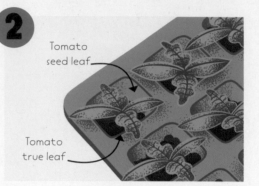

Tomato seed leaf

Tomato true leaf

When leaves sprout, remove the cover. Once the seedlings have a set of scalloped-edged leaves, called true leaves, it's time to move them into small pots filled with potting mix.

4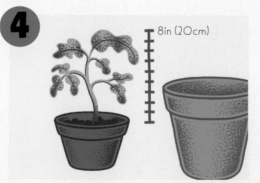

8in (20cm)

When the weather is mild enough and the tomato plants are about 6-8in (15-20cm) tall, move them into bigger pots or plant them in the garden in a sunny, but sheltered place.

5

Side shoot

Tie each plant to a bamboo stake for support. Pinch out any side shoots that appear between a leaf and the main stem as the plants grow.

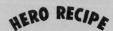

TOP TIP!

Tomatoes taste sweeter when picked in the morning because of how the tomato plants store sugars overnight.

3

Gently lift the seedlings out of the seed tray and transfer each one to its own pot. The potting mix should come up to their first set of leaves. Keep the seedlings in a sunny position indoors and water regularly.

Not all of the tomatoes will ripen at the same time

6 HARVEST TIME!

Pick the cherry tomatoes in 7–12 weeks. When ready, they will be bright red and the fruit, when twisted, should fall off the plant easily.

Add more bamboo stakes to support the tomato plant as it grows.

SEED SAVING

Scoop out the seeds from a tomato, put them in a jar, and cover with water. After five days, a film will form. Rinse the seeds in a strainer and dry them out on paper towels. When they are totally dry, store them in a cool, dark place.

Make sure your potatoes are fully covered by soil and mulch. This protects the potatoes from sunlight. Sunlight turns potatoes green and they become toxic.

Grow UNDERGROUND

Did you know that some of the tastiest veggies grow under the soil? Think of the smell of roasted garlic or of yummy potatoes, which can be boiled or turned into French fries or mashed potatoes. Start digging!

Grow NEW POTATOES

Potato plants grow from store-bought seed potatoes, which have been grown to be replanted. You can grow purple potatoes following these steps, too!

Plant in spring/summer/fall

Grow in well-drained sandy loam soil, pH 5.8-6.5

Grow in a sunny place

You will need

- 3-4 seed potatoes
- Soft fruit tray
- Potting mix
- Large pot 24in (60cm) deep
- Mulch

HERO RECIPE

Potato and spinach salad

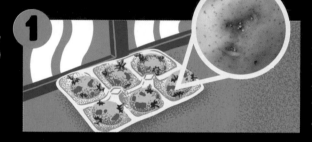

1 Before planting, some people "chit" the seed potatoes by placing them in the soft fruit tray with their spots (eyes) facing upward. Leave them in a light, cool place until their eyes start sprouting.

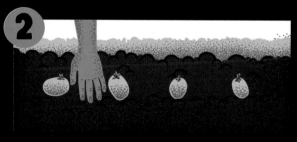

2 Add 4in (10cm) of potting mix to the large pot. Plant the seed potatoes a hand's width apart, with their sprouting eyes pointing up. Cover with 4in (10cm) of potting mix. Top with 2in (5cm) of mulch. Water regularly.

3 When shoots appear, cover them by adding more potting mix or mulch—this is called earthing up. Repeat this as the plants grow. Keep well watered, but not wet.

HARVEST TIME!

4 When the leaves turn yellow and begin to die, the potatoes are ready. This is usually after 12 weeks. Ask an adult to help you dig out the potatoes. It's a little like finding buried treasure.

Remove any spear-shaped stems on your garlic plants to encourage the bulbs to grow bigger. These can then be eaten.

WE GROW UNDERGROUND, TOO!

Beets

Carrots

Turmeric

Onions

Grow GARLIC

A garlic bulb, also known as a head, is divided into smaller parts, known as cloves. You can grow a whole new head of garlic from a single clove!

Plant in spring/fall

Grow in well-drained sandy loam soil, pH 6-7

Grow in a sunny place

You will need

- Large pot
  6in (15cm) wide,
  12in (30cm) deep
- Potting mix
- 3 garlic cloves

HERO RECIPE

Pull-apart garlic bread and garlicky bruschetta

1

Fill the large pot with potting mix. Place the cloves in the pot, about 4in (10cm) apart, with the flat base of each clove facing down and the pointed ends reaching toward the sky.

2

Cover with 1¼in (3cm) of potting mix and water well. When shoots start to grow, you don't need to cover (earth) them like you do with potatoes.

3

Water often when the weather is drier. Once the bulbs have grown, reduce watering to once a week. Check the bulbs by scraping off some of the potting mix.

4 HARVEST TIME!

Garlic is ready when the leaves turn yellow, usually after about 8-9 months. Remove the potting mix from the top of each bulb and gently pull the bulbs up by their stems. Hang them in a cool, dry place to store.

Grow BRASSICAS

Brassica is the Latin word for cabbage, but this family of plants also includes radish, kale, broccoli, and arugula. Brassicas can be spotted by their heart-shaped first set of leaves and seed pods that look like worms.

Brassicas are great cover crops. They produce hundreds of seeds, which grow into seedlings that stop the soil from drying out on windy or sunny days and keep it full of life.

Grow TUSCAN KALE

Did you know that there are more than 20 types of kale, all with unique leaves, colors, and flavors? Tuscan is a variety of kale with dark, spoon-shaped leaves.

Plant in spring

Grow in well-drained loam or sandy loam soil, pH 6-7.5

Grow in a sunny place

You will need

- Small pot
- Potting mix
- 3-4 Tuscan kale seeds
- Large pot 6½ gal (30 liters) or bigger
- Trowel
- Mulch

Brassicas are also known as "cruciferous" vegetables because their flowers have four petals in a cross shape.

1

Fill the small pot with potting mix, add 3-4 Tuscan kale seeds, then cover with more mix. Water well and place on a sunny windowsill.

2

Once the kale plants start to sprout, move them outdoors into the large pot filled with 10-12in (25-30cm) of potting mix. Using the trowel, make 3-4 holes that are deep enough to fit the plant's roots. Plant a seedling per hole.

3

Add mulch around the seedlings and water regularly.

4
HARVEST TIME!

"Cut-and-come-again" is a harvest method that works well for brassicas. As the plants grow, remove what you need from them to get longer and bigger harvests. Pick the lower leaves of the kale plants when they are around 8in (20cm) long. Allow the top leaves to grow.

One size
FITS ALL (almost)

Most vegetables in the brassica family
can be planted at the same time using
a similar method. Follow the steps
for growing Tuscan kale and,
with a few changes, you
can also have arugula
and broccolini.

Grow arugula

Arugulas' peppery leaves are
tasty in salads, and their white
flowers with purple veins help
attract useful pollinators.

As with kale, plant arugula seeds in
the spring in a small pot of potting
mix, spacing the seeds about 1in (3cm)
apart. Let the plants grow in the
small pot and begin picking their
top and outer leaves after 6 weeks.
Keep harvesting until the plants
produce flowers.

Grow broccolini

Broccolini has large roots, called
taproots, that grow deep into
the soil, so make sure to give the
plants lots of room to grow.

As with kale, start broccolini off in
the spring in small pots of potting
mix and place the pots on a
windowsill. Move the seedlings into
the large pot of potting mix or plant
in the ground. Space plants 32in
(80cm) apart and harvest before
the plant's flower opens. Cut the
florets an inch or so from each stem.

Grow CUCURBITS

Some of the most popular crops in the world belong to a family of veggies called cucurbits. These include pumpkins and melons, as well as two that we really love to grow—butternut squash and zucchini! The key to successful growing is to get the conditions right.

Cucurbits love the heat, so grow them somewhere sunny. They are also thirsty and hungry plants, which means they need lots of water and compost.

The bright yellow flowers attract pollinators, which allow the plant to grow more zucchini.

Grow ZUCCHINI

In the garden, zucchini soak up the sun's rays. In the kitchen, they are flavor sponges that soak up delicious seasonings.

Plant in spring/summer

Grow in well-drained loam soil, pH 6-7

Grow in a sunny place

You will need

- Small pot 2-4in (5-10cm) deep
- Potting mix
- Zucchini seed
- Large pot 6½ gal (30 liter) or bigger
- Well-rotted manure
- Sharp knife or pruners

1 Fill the small pot with potting mix. Plant 1 zucchini seed per pot and cover with ½-¾in (1-2cm) potting mix. Water well. Place in a sunny spot indoors.

2 Water the plant regularly. In warm weather, sprouts should appear between 5-9 days.

3 When the plant has 6 or more true leaves, it can be moved into the large pot filled with potting mix or directly into the ground. As the plant grows, cover the mix with well-rotted manure.

HARVEST TIME!

4 Pick zucchini when they are roughly 4-6in (10-15cm) long. Ask an adult to use the sharp knife or pruners to cut the stem about 1in (2.5cm) above the top of the fruit.

TOP TIP!

Although butternut squash and zucchini are part of the same family and require similar growing conditions, they shouldn't be grown close together. They'll compete for food, water, and space.

Squash is a heavy veggie, so ask an adult for help before harvesting.

Zucchini make big bushy plants, while squash like to spread and climb. This makes them fantastic plants for protecting the soil.

Grow
BUTTERNUT SQUASH

Unlike zucchini, butternut squash tends to have long vines that can cover a lot of ground. These arms can be trained to grow vertically.

FUN FACT!

The more zucchini you pick, the more the plant will produce. It's like magic!

1

Plant butternut squash seeds in spring or summer, then follow steps 1, 2, and 3 for growing zucchini.

Butternut squash take longer to ripen than zucchini. Pick them in the fall when they are an even tan color, their skin is hard, and their stems are turning brown. Ask an adult to cut off the fruit, leaving 2–2½in (5–6cm) of stem still attached.

BIODIVERSITY BADGE

There are lots of varieties of zucchini. We like to grow Rugosa Friulana zucchini. These have a firm texture, a fun yellow color, and are naturally pest-resistant. They are often called the ugly zucchini, but their taste more than makes up for their looks.

Plant in late spring

Grow in well-drained loam soil, pH 6–6.8

Grow in a sunny place

You will need

- Small pots 4in (10cm) deep
- Potting mix
- Corn seeds
- Large pot 6½ gal (30 liters) or bigger

1 Fill small pots with at least 2½–3in (6–8cm) of potting mix. Plant 1 seed per pot, about ¾–1in (2–3cm) deep in the potting mix, then water. Keep in a warm place and water well for 2 weeks.

2 When the corn plants are about 3–6in (8–15cm) tall, move them into the large pot filled with potting mix or directly into the ground. Plant in a grid formation to help with pollination.

FUN FACT!

Most plants rely on animals such as Halle Honeybee to spread their pollen. But corn plants are pollinated by the wind!

3 If the weather is warm, you'll need to water the plants twice a week for roughly 8–10 weeks.

4 Corn is ripe and ready when the corn silks (long, stringlike strands) turn brown and the corn kernels are plump. To pick, twist the corncobs downward. They should come off the stalks easily.

Grow CORN

Corn is a delicious fruit. It's a fruit because the part that is eaten comes from its flower. Corn is yummy in many ways: ground up, popped, or on the cob.

HERO RECIPE
Corn soup and roasted corn ribs

BIODIVERSITY BADGE

There are many varieties of corn. Heirloom seeds, which come from plants you have had for a long time, are a great way to gain your biodiversity badge.

FIESTA

Fiesta corn adds lots of color to your garden and plate. It's best for cooking over a long time in stews.

PEACHES AND CREAM

Peaches and cream corn has a very sweet flavor. In warm weather, it is ready to harvest in 65 days.

Most corncobs have 16 rows, and all corncobs have an even number of rows.

TOP TIP!

Corn is sweetest when picked in the morning, since the plants produce more sugars during the night.

Did you know that corn orginated in Mexico, but humans have been eating it across the world for thousands of years?

Most corn is yellow, but some is multicolored.

Grow PODDED VEGETABLES

Peas, chickpeas, and beans are all podded vegetables, which means that the seeds of these plants form inside pods. Podded vegetables are also known as legumes or pulses, and you can grow different types for eating fresh, or dried to enjoy later.

Grow BORLOTTI BEANS

If you grow these beans alongside corn, you won't need a bamboo structure to support them. The beans will climb up the corn instead.

Plant in spring

Grow in loam soil, pH 6–7

Grow in a sunny place

You will need

- 6 borlotti or cranberry beans
- 6 small pots at least 3in (8cm) deep
- Potting mix
- Clear plastic bags
- 4 bamboo stakes
- Large, deep pot 12in (30cm) wide
- String
- Trowel
- Mulch

1 Sow seeds indoors in small pots filled with potting mix. Plant each borlotti or cranberry bean 2in (5cm) deep. Place on a sunny windowsill, cover with the plastic bag, and water well.

2 Put 4 bamboo stakes into the large pot of potting mix outdoors and tie them together near the top. Using the trowel, make 6 holes in the mix near the bottom of each stake.

3 When the weather is mild, move the seedlings outside. Put them in the holes. Then tie each seedling to its nearest stake to help the beans grow upward.

4 Cover the potting mix with mulch, such as leaves, wood chips, or grass clippings. Keep the plants well watered.

HERO RECIPE

Mexican mole beans

5 **HARVEST TIME!**

Beans should be ready in 60–70 days. To eat them fresh, pick your bean pods when they are long and tender. Otherwise, wait until the bean pods start to dry out, then pop the beans out and leave them on a tray to dry fully. When they're hard, store them in an airtight container.

Beans are grown and eaten on almost every continent on Earth! Each country has its own special way of cooking beans, so you can't get bored with them.

GOOD GAS

Beans can give you gas, but that's good! They show that your gut is working well and getting rid of unwanted stuff. Next time you have wind after eating beans, remember it's because your gut is doing its job!

Sprout CHICKPEAS

Some beans can be sprouted before eating them. This is a little trick that supercharges the beans with nutrients and makes them easier for your tummy to digest.

Makes 7oz (200g)

2-4 days

Tools

- Large bowl
- Strainer or colander
- Metal spoon
- Dish towel

Ingredients

- 3oz (85g) dried organic chickpeas
- Juice of 1 large lemon

1 Place the dried chickpeas in the large bowl and cover with water. Put in a cool, dark place and leave to soak for around 12 hrs, or overnight.

2 After 12 hrs, place the chickpeas in the strainer or colander and rinse well under fresh, cold water.

3 Put the chickpeas back into the bowl and pour the lemon juice over the top. Stir well with the metal spoon or your hands and then drain and rinse again.

4 Spread the chickpeas in the strainer or colander and rest it over the bowl. Cover with the dish towel for 12 hrs, or 1 day.

5 Repeat stage 2 for 2-4 days, twice a day, until you see a tail (root) ½-¾in (1-2cm) long. The sprouted chickpeas are ready and should smell fresh.

HERO RECIPE

Magic chickpea hummus

Eating different colored beans can help your gut, so be sure to try them all!

Grow LEAFY VEGETABLES

Leafy vegetables are something we grow primarily for their edible leaves or stems. This is quite a big group of plants, but our favorites, amaranth and spinach, are easy-to-grow and nutritious. Other tasty examples include chard and lettuce.

Grow SPINACH

Meet spinach, the super leaf! This green hero doesn't like to wait around, so you can grow bundles of it quickly.

 Plant in late spring/early fall

 Grow in loam soil, pH 6-7

Grow in part sun, part shade

You will need

- Trough 24in (60cm) long
- Potting mix
- Well-rotted manure (optional)
- Spinach seeds

HERO RECIPE

Spinach and leek tart

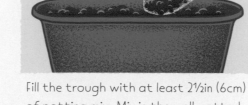

1 Fill the trough with at least 2½in (6cm) of potting mix. Mix in the well-rotted manure (if using).

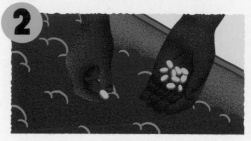

2 Plant spinach seeds 1in (2.5cm) deep in the potting mix and about 8in (20cm) apart.

3 Water regularly—spinach plants will start to flower and stop growing tasty leaves if they get too dry.

4 HARVEST TIME!

Treat spinach as a cut-and-come-again plant. When the plants have roughly 6 leaves, start picking the outer leaves, letting the ones in the center grow, so they keep producing leaves for longer.

Grow AMARANTH

Known as "callaloo" in parts of the Caribbean, amaranth is a leafy green and a grain. You can eat its leaves, its red, foxtail plume of flowers, and the seeds inside the flowers!

Plant in spring

Grow in well-drained sandy soil, pH 6-7

Grow in a sunny place

You will need

- Potting mix
- Small pot
- Amaranth seeds
- Clear plastic bag
- Large pot 6½ gal (30 liters) or bigger
- Paper bag
- 2 bowls

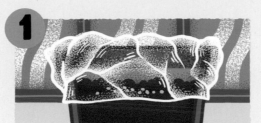

1 Add 2½in (6cm) of potting mix to the small pot. Scatter a few seeds on top, water, then cover with the plastic bag. Place on a sunny windowsill and water for 1 week. Remove the bag when leaves appear.

2 Once the plants sprout, thin them out so each plant is 2-4in (5-10cm) apart. Add the thinned seedlings as microgreens in a salad. As the plants grow, continue removing some leaves to thin them out.

3 At 3-4 weeks (provided there is no frost), transfer the amaranth plants into the large pot filled with potting mix. Once it's happy, amaranth grows very fast.

4 HARVEST TIME! Use the cut-and-come-again method to harvest the leaves. Pinch out the top leaves to encourage bushy, leafy plants. Reserve 1 plant to harvest the seeds from. Do not pick leaves from the plant.

5 HARVEST TIME! Harvest the seeds when the flowers dry out. Cut the flower stalks and place in the paper bag to dry. Go outside to shake the seeds into the bowl then tip them into another bowl. Pass the seeds between the bowls 10 times. This is called winnowing and it helps remove flowers and chaff (coverings) from the seeds.

Some seeds might fall on the ground, so only winnow in a place you're happy for more flowers to sprout.

Amaranth flowers were used to make candied cherries red.

Amaranth seeds are full of calcium and magnesium.

HERO RECIPE
Amaranth choc chip cookies and amaranth granola

BIODIVERSITY BADGE

Many people think of leafy vegetables as being green, but they can also come in red, purple, and even white!

RED AMARANTH   **PURPLE KALE**   **BOK CHOY**

Grow RASPBERRIES

Grow blackberries in pots, otherwise they can take over!

Did you know that raspberries (and blackberries) are not actually berries? In fact, they're made up of lots of tiny berries grouped together. These fruits are known as "aggregate fruits," as each tiny berry has its own seed.

Raspberry plants need to be protected from strong winds, so plant them in sheltered areas.

Plant in fall

Grow in loam soil, pH 6-6.5

Grow in part sun, part shade

You will need

- 1-year-old fall-fruiting raspberry cane (stem of the plant)
- Bucket
- Large pot at least 24in (60cm) wide
- Potting mix
- Bamboo stake
- String
- Mulch

1 Soak the roots of the raspberry cane in the bucket of water for 1 hr before planting.

2 Meanwhile, fill the large pot with potting mix. Make a hole in the center that is wide and deep enough to hold the plant's roots. Insert the bamboo stake next to this hole.

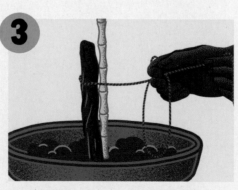

3 Plant the raspberry cane in the hole and then cut it down to 10in (25cm) above soil level. Tie the plant to the bamboo stake to keep it upright as it grows.

4 Spread a 2-4in (5-10cm) layer of mulch over the potting soil. Water your raspberry plant regularly while it is fruiting.

HERO RECIPE

Berry cobbler

Raspberries come in lots of different colors. They can be black, red, yellow, purple, or pink!

Blackberries can be grown in a similar way to raspberries, but don't plant them close together. They'll compete for nutrients and may spread diseases to each other.

TOP TIP!

Trim your raspberry plant at the end of fall. It will fruit again in the following summer, then it can be composted.

Raspberries turn from brown to yellow to red as they ripen.

5 HARVEST TIME!

Using a 1-year-old raspberry cane should give you fruit from summer until early fall. When the raspberries look plump and juicy and can be picked easily, they're ready to harvest.

PLATE

Now, get ready for the tasty part—cooking. Discover chef secrets so you can prepare food like a pro. Then explore yummy recipes that include the hero ingredients you've grown and harvested.

COOKING equipment

Here are the tools you'll need for the recipes. Make sure you have the right equipment ready before cooking.

HERO INGREDIENT
Basil

This icon tells you which of the ingredients you've grown is the star of the meal.

Teaspoon Tablespoon Wooden spoon Metal spoon Fork Bread knife Sharp knife Blunt table knife Peeler

Ladle Spatula Slotted spoon Garlic press Pizza cutter Oven mitts Tongs Grater

Skillet Saucepan Ridged grill pan Colander Pizza pan Baking dish

Strainer/ sifter Rolling pin Hand whisk Baking beans Wire rack Foil

Cupcake pan and paper cases Baking pan Baking sheet Blender Food processor Electric mixer

Paper towels Jar with lid Parchment paper Cutting board Cut-resistant gloves Handheld blender Pie pan

Look at the information on these icons before you start a recipe.

SERVING SIZE

This lists the number of portions a recipe makes or how many people it serves.

PREPARATION TIME

This tells you how many minutes and hours a recipe will take to prepare. It includes times for extra preparation, such as chilling and rising.

COOKING TIME

This tells you how long it will take to cook a dish.

Kitchen KNOW-HOW

Before you get started making the yummy recipes in this book, there are certain cooking techniques you'll need to master. Here are some useful steps and explanations to help you become a superchef in no time.

Kitchen terms

⚠ BLEND
Mixing ingredients together in a food processor or blender until combined

⚠ CHOP
Using a knife to cut ingredients into smaller pieces

COAT
Covering food with a wet or dry coating, such as batter or bread crumbs

COOL
Placing ingredients, or a dish you've made, in the fridge to keep it chilled

⚠ CRUSH
Smashing food into small pieces using your hands or other equipment

PREPARE

Every recipe requires some preparation. Follow these instructions so you can prep like a professional.

Grease a dish
Use parchment paper or a paper towel to spread a thin, slippery layer of olive oil over the inside of the pie pan (or muffin pan or bowl)—this stops the food from sticking to the dish!

Flax "egg"
A flax "egg" is a great egg replacement. It's made with 3 tbsp flax seeds and 3 tbsp water. Let it sit for 10 mins before using. It's packed full of omega-3 and amino acids, so it's good for your brain and muscles!

Sift

Shake dry, powdered ingredients, such as flour, through a sifter to get rid of lumps and to add air.

Line a baking pan or sheet

 **1** Lay out some parchment paper and draw around your pan or sheet. Carefully cut out your shape.

 **2** Place your paper in the pan or on the sheet. Fold at the corners, if needed, and snip off any excess.

Roll out

Put a piece of parchment paper over your dough, place a rolling pin over the parchment, and roll to flatten the dough.

Knead

 **1** Flour your surface before you start. Use the heel of your hand to push the dough away from you.

 **2** Next, fold the squashed end of the dough over and turn the whole piece around.

 **3** Repeat the squashing, folding, and turning until the dough is soft and smooth.

DE-STEM
Removing the leaves of a sprig (stem) by dragging your fingers down it

⚠️ **DICE**
Using a knife to cut food into small cubes

⚠️ **DRAIN**
Removing liquid by pouring ingredients through a colander or strainer

⚠️ **GRATE**
Shredding an ingredient into small pieces by rubbing it against a grater

JUICE
Squeezing the liquid out of fruits or vegetables

⚠️ **MELT**
Applying heat to change a food, such as coconut oil or butter, from solid to liquid in either the microwave, using a heatproof bowl, or in a saucepan on the stovetop

⚠️ **MIX**
Combining ingredients together, by hand or with equipment

⚠️ **PEEL**
Removing the skin from an ingredient by dragging a peeler across it

⚠️ **SLICE**
Using a knife to cut ingredients into strips

⚠️ **TOAST**
Browning ingredients with a dry heat

TOSS
Shaking or mixing small pieces of food together with a sauce or dressing

⚠️ **WHISK**
Whipping up ingredients, using a whisk and a quick flick of the wrist, to introduce air into the mixture

⚠️ **ZEST**
Scraping the outer peel of a citrus fruit, to use the shavings in a recipe

COOK

Cooking your food involves heat, so it's important to have an adult's help and supervision on the following cooking methods.

Boil
Heat food on high heat and allow bubbles to dance vigorously in your pan. Keep watch and turn the heat down if the bubbles get overexcited and boil over the edge of the pan.

Sauté
Sauté is a fancy word for cooking food in a skillet with a little bit of oil. This is also known as frying. Keep the food moving around in the pan so it doesn't burn!

Simmer

Heat food on low heat to make gentle bubbles.

Broil

The heat comes from above, so food needs to be turned during broiling.

Bake

Cooking food in an oven is baking. Muffins, cookies, and tarts are all baked.

Blind-bake

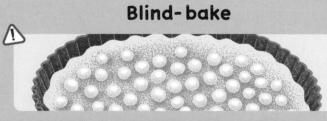

Bake the pie crust before adding the filling. Line the crust with parchment paper and half-fill it with baking beans, then put in the oven to bake.

INGREDIENT *swaps*

What an ingredient can do for your body depends on what it is and how you use it. Different varieties of ingredients have special powers. Before you go food shopping, look at these ideas to help your family choose their ingredients.

Flours

WE USE: Spelt flour, chickpea flour, and buckwheat flour.

WHY: They are high in fiber, which gut bacteria love, and they give a slow, steady energy release.

SPELT FLOUR

CHICKPEA FLOUR

BUCKWHEAT FLOUR

Oils

WE USE: Coconut oil and extra virgin olive oil.

WHY: These oils are great to use in cooking. Coconut oil has a high smoke point, and olive oil has a good omega-3 to omega-6 balance.

COCONUT OIL

OLIVE OIL

Pasta

WE USE: Whole wheat pasta and spelt pasta.

WHY: These contain lots of vitamins and minerals, as well as tummy-friendly fiber. They also give you energy that lasts throughout the day.

WHOLE WHEAT PASTA

SPELT PASTA

Salts

WE USE: Pink Himalayan salt, sea salt, and even seaweed.

WHY: Natural salts contain more minerals than table salt. Seaweed has a naturally salty flavor and is a great source of iodine. Next time you're boiling pasta, add some seaweed to the pan.

Sweeteners

WE USE: Coconut sugar, dates, agave syrup, and ripe fruits.

WHY: Fruits are sweet, but they also contain valuable vitamins and minerals. They provide a slow release of energy throughout the day.

RIPE FRUITS

PINK HIMALAYAN SALT

SEA SALT

SEAWEED

COCONUT SUGAR

DATES

AGAVE SYRUP

TOP TIP!

When cooking with dried legumes, soak them before using. For flours such as chickpea flour, soak for 1 hr and for beans soak for 24 hrs. This makes them easier to digest.

PANTRY *power*

A pantry is a space for cold ingredients that don't need to be kept in the fridge.

RED LENTILS

OATS

CHICKPEAS

CHICKPEAS

CHICKPEAS

CAROB SYRUP

VANILLA EXTRACT

ARTICHOKE HEARTS

THYME

SMOKED PAPRIKA

CORIANDER

CUMIN

OREGANO

NUTMEG

TARRAGON

CARDAMOM

BLACK PEPPER

BAY LEAVES

PINE NUTS

PUMPKIN SEEDS

FLAX SEEDS

Basil PESTO PASTA

Every variety of basil grows well in the heat, but most types don't cook well. The basil in this pesto sauce is raw, so the dish is extra fresh and full of flavor.

•Level•
EASY
•Rating•

Serves 4   10 mins   15 mins

Tools

- Skillet
- Food processor
- Large saucepan
- Colander

Ingredients

- 2 large garlic cloves, unpeeled
- ⅓ cup pumpkin seeds or pine nuts
- 3¾ cups fresh basil leaves
- 1 tsp maple or carob syrup
- 1 cup olive oil
- Salt and freshly ground black pepper
- ¼ cup marinated artichoke hearts (optional)
- 11oz (325g) pasta

Eating basil can boost your immune system, which helps you fight off illness. Leafy greens have the power to do that!

1 Ask an adult to roast the garlic and pumpkin seeds or pine nuts in the skillet over medium-high heat for 5 mins. The garlic and nuts will turn golden. The pumpkin seeds will start to pop.

2 Transfer into the food processor and add the basil leaves, maple or carob syrup, olive oil, salt and pepper, as well as the artichoke hearts (if using).

3 Blend everything until it forms a lumpy paste. A lumpy texture is great, so try not to blend the mixture too much.

4 Ask an adult to boil slightly salted water in the large saucepan. Add the pasta when the water is boiling and cook for 8-10 mins, or follow the instructions on the package.

5 Ask an adult to use the colander to drain the pasta carefully. Return the pasta to the pan and stir in the pesto sauce. Serve while hot.

Change IT UP!

Try variations of this classic pesto pasta by adding thyme or lemon to give it a floral or zesty twist.

THYME PESTO

Follow the recipe for Basil Pesto Pasta and, at step 2, add 2 tbsp of thyme leaves, stems removed.

LEMONY PESTO

Follow the recipe for Basil Pesto Pasta and, at step 2, add the finely grated zest of ½ lemon and the juice of 1 lemon. The lemon will help keep the dish fresh for longer.

TOP TIP!

Store pesto in an airtight container in the fridge for up to 1 week. Make sure the pesto is covered in oil to preserve its full flavor.

Tomato PIZZA

Juicy and sweet cherry tomatoes are the hero ingredient in this pizza sauce. Once you've mastered the pizza dough, cover it with your special sauce and use whatever combination of toppings you like.

•Level•
MEDIUM
•Rating•

  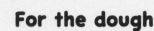

Makes 4   20 mins, plus 2 hrs rising   13–20 mins

Tools

- 2 large bowls
- Metal spoon
- Clean, damp cloth or plastic wrap
- Blender
- Medium saucepan
- Wooden spoon
- Rolling pin
- 4 pizza pans or stones
- Oven mitts
- Pizza cutter
- Cutting board

For the dough

- 4½ cups white spelt flour, plus extra for dusting
- 1½ tsp active dry yeast
- 1 tsp salt
- 3⅓ cups lukewarm water
- Olive oil, for greasing

For the tomato sauce

- 1lb 2oz (500g) cherry tomatoes
- 3 dates, pitted (optional)
- 2 garlic cloves, peeled
- 2 tbsp dried oregano

Suggested toppings

- Mushrooms, thinly sliced
- Yellow, orange, and red bell peppers, thinly sliced
- Handful of kale leaves, finely sliced (stems removed)
- Olive oil, for drizzling
- Handful of fresh basil leaves, to serve

1 In 1 of the large bowls, use the metal spoon to mix together the flour, yeast, salt, and water until they form a dough.

2 On a lightly floured surface, knead the dough, stretching and pulling as you go, for 2–3 mins, or until the dough feels smooth. Form the dough into a large ball.

3 Lightly grease the other bowl with oil, then add the dough. Cover with the damp cloth or plastic wrap and leave to rise in a warm place for 2 hrs, or until the dough has doubled in size.

⚠4 Ask an adult to whiz all the tomato sauce ingredients in the blender, until smooth. Pour the sauce in the saucepan and simmer gently for 3–4 mins, or until it's thick enough to coat the back of the wooden spoon.

⚠5 Ask an adult to preheat the oven to 475°F (240°C). Lightly punch down the risen dough, then divide it into 4 equal pieces. Lightly knead each piece on a floured surface, before rolling them out into a 10–12in (25–30cm) circle. Place the pizza dough on the pizza pans or stones.

I protect tomato plants in the garden. You can protect tomatoes in the kitchen. Store your sauce in a container in the fridge for 1 week, or freeze it for up to 1 month.

6 Using the back of the wooden spoon, spread tomato sauce over each crust, leaving a small border around the edge. Add toppings to each pizza and drizzle with the olive oil.

 7 Cook the pizzas in batches. Ask an adult to place 2 pizzas onto separate oven racks. Cook for 5-8 mins, or until the crusts are crispy and risen. Swap the pizzas around on the racks halfway through baking. Top with the basil leaves, then ask an adult to slice the pizzas on the cutting board.

TOP TIP!

Make another batch of this super special tomato sauce to add to your zucchini lasagna or as a sauce for chips.

RANCH DRESSING

MARINARA SAUCE

HERO INGREDIENT
Garlic

If you fry your garlic before using it, the taste will be less powerful, but just as delicious.

PULL-APART *garlic* BREAD

Did you know that garlic is sometimes called the stinking rose? When it's cooked, this strong scented veggie becomes yummy for your tummy!

•Level• **EASY** •Rating•

Serves 4   10 mins   7–10 mins

Tools

- Bread knife
- Cutting board
- Garlic press
- Small bowl
- Metal spoon
- Small skillet
- Wooden spoon
- Baking sheet
- Oven mitts

Ingredients

- 1 baguette, partly baked
- ½ small garlic bulb
- ¼ cup olive oil or butter of your choice
- ¼ cup fresh flat-leaf parsley, finely chopped
- ½ tsp salt

1 Ask an adult to preheat the oven to 400°F (200°C) and then use the bread knife to slice the baguette carefully, making sure to cut only three-quarters of the way down, so the bread stays intact at the bottom.

2 Crush the garlic into the small bowl. Add the olive oil or butter, parsley, and salt. Mix everything with the metal spoon.

3 Ask an adult to sauté this mixture in the skillet on medium heat, until the garlic is golden. Then evenly coat the inside of each slice with the mixture.

4 Place the baguette on the baking sheet and sprinkle it with water. Ask an adult to place the sheet in the oven and bake for 7–10 mins, or until golden brown. The garlic mixture should bubble.

5 Let the bread rest until it is cool enough to handle, then pull each slice apart to serve.

Garlicky BRUSCHETTA

Garlic is a confident character and can be found in most kitchens. It complements a lot of meals, but goes well with tomatoes, basil, and parsley.

TOP TIP!

To remove the strong smell of garlic from your fingers, rub them on a stainless steel spoon under cold running water.

Serves 2   3 mins   3 mins

Tools

- Ridged grill pan
- Tongs
- Sharp knife
- Cutting board
- Metal spoon

Ingredients

- 4 slices ciabatta/baguette
- 1 large tomato
- 2 garlic cloves
- Drizzle of olive oil
- Salt
- Fresh basil leaves, to garnish

⚠ 1 Place the ciabatta slices on the ridged grill pan. Ask an adult to carefully toast the pieces of bread on both sides, until golden brown.

⚠ 2 Ask an adult to carefully slice the large tomato in half. Rub 1 side of each slice of bread with the garlic and tomato so it soaks up all of the flavor.

⚠ 3 An adult should then slice the 2 halves of the tomato into small chunks. Spoon the chunks onto the slices of bread.

4 Before serving, drizzle olive oil on top and season with salt. Garnish with the basil leaves.

Garlic means "spear leek" in Old English, because it looks like a leek with a spearhead when it grows! It tastes a little like leek, too.

The dressing will keep fresh in the fridge for up to 1 week.

FLOWER-POWERED
arugula AND *violet* SALAD

Eating salads, such as this one with arugula, is a healthy way to keep your tummy bacteria well-fed. When bacteria are happy, they do their best job of helping your body absorb vitamins and minerals.

•Level•
EASY
•Rating•

Serves 4   5 mins   5 mins

Tools

- Small skillet
- Jar with lid
- Bowl

For the salad

- 2 tbsp pumpkin seeds
- 1¼ cup arugula leaves
- Handful of lamb's lettuce or watercress
- Sprinkle of violets or any other edible flower, to serve (optional)

For the dressing

- ¾ cup extra virgin olive oil
- 2 tbsp lemon juice
- 2 tbsp cider vinegar
- 1 tsp agave or maple syrup
- 1 tsp salt
- 1 tbsp blueberry or raspberry puree (optional)

It's important to remember that not all flowers are edible, so ask an adult for help in finding ones that are.

1 Ask an adult to toast the pumpkin seeds in the skillet over medium heat. You don't need oil. Once they start to pop and you can smell the nutty oils being released, it's time to take the seeds off the stovetop.

2 To make your salad dressing, add the oil, lemon juice, cider vinegar, syrup, and salt to the jar. At this stage, you can also add the berry puree to the dressing (if using). Put the lid on the jar and shake well—use those muscles to mix the dressing!

3 Put the leafy greens into the bowl and pour half of the dressing over them. They should be lightly coated so they have a sheen. Store the leftover dressing in the fridge.

4 Scatter the seeds and edible flowers on top (if using). Flowers add color and transform your salad into a work of art!

Potato AND spinach SALAD

Level EASY Rating

Add a range of salad greens, such as iron-rich spinach, into a potato salad to add lots of green goodness to a meal. This recipe is perfect as a side dish.

Serves 6   10 mins   10 mins

Tools

- Large saucepan
- Fork
- Jar with lid
- Colander
- Serving bowl

For the salad

- 2lb (900g) new potatoes (or purple potatoes), cut into 1in (2.5cm) chunks
- 1¼ cup arugula leaves
- Handful of spinach leaves

For the dressing

- ½ tsp fresh tarragon leaves (or ½ tsp fresh rosemary), chopped
- 1 green onion, finely sliced
- 2 tbsp mayonnaise of your choice
- 1 tbsp lemon juice
- ½ tsp salt
- Freshly ground black pepper, to taste

1 Ask an adult to bring a pan of lightly salted water to a boil. Carefully add the potatoes and boil for 10 mins, or until the fork can easily pierce a potato.

2 To make the dressing, place the herbs, green onion, mayonnaise, lemon juice, salt, and pepper in the jar. Make sure the lid is on tight, turn on your favorite music, and shake the jar to the rhythm until the ingredients are well mixed.

3 Ask an adult to drain the potatoes and place them in the serving bowl.

4 Once the potatoes have cooled, drizzle the dressing over them. Scatter the arugula and spinach over the salad for a beautiful, bright-green dish.

TOP TIP!

To make your salads sing, you need the perfect dressing. This is made from a mixture of salty, fatty (oil), sweet (agave or maple syrup), and acidic (lemon juice) ingredients.

Purple potatoes have a similar texture to new potatoes.

Let the potatoes cool before adding the leaves, otherwise they'll wilt.

Remember to wash your leafy greens well to make sure no bugs are hiding in there!

TOP TIP!

Garnish your salad with red or yellow nasturtium flowers to make it a real showstopper. Only some flowers are edible, so check with an adult that the ones you pick are.

CHARRED *broccolini* SALAD

•Level•
EASY
•Rating•

Broccolini can be eaten raw, boiled, fried, or, as in this recipe... charred! Charring broccolini brings out its tasty flavor and keeps all of its immune boosting goodness in.

Serves 2-3   8 mins   7-10 mins

Tools

- Sharp knife
- Cutting board
- Skillet with lid
- Tongs
- Measuring cup
- Handheld blender
- Serving plate
- Salad servers

For the salad

- 7oz (200g) broccolini
- 2 tbsp olive oil
- 1 garlic clove, crushed (optional)
- ¼ tsp salt
- Edible nasturtium flowers, to garnish (optional)

For the dressing

- ¾ cup arugula leaves, plus extra to garnish
- 3 tbsp olive oil
- ½ tsp grated orange zest
- 1½ tbsp orange juice
- ½ tsp Dijon mustard
- ½ tsp agave or maple syrup
- ¼ tsp salt

1 Ask an adult to use the sharp knife to cut the thick stem off each broccolini. Carefully separate any florets into single heads that are all similar in size.

2 Ask an adult to heat the olive oil in the skillet over high heat. Using the tongs, add the broccolini to the skillet. Put the lid on the skillet, reduce the heat to medium, and let it sizzle.

3 Cook for about 5 mins, until the broccolini is slightly charred on one side, then carefully flip it and cook the other side for another 2 mins, or until it is equally charred.

4 At this point, add the garlic to the skillet (if using), taking care not to burn it. Then season with salt and set aside.

5 Place all of the ingredients for the dressing into the measuring cup and blend until smooth.

6 Transfer the broccolini onto the serving plate. Pour the dressing over the top and toss everything together with the salad servers. Garnish with the arugula leaves and nasturtium flowers (if using).

⚠ *Change* IT UP!

For a veggie-packed meal, add 7oz (200g) each of cabbage and cauliflower. Char them before the broccolini, and double the salad dressing quantities to cover all the vegetables.

CABBAGE

ROMANESCO CAULIFLOWER

Carefully chop the cabbage into wedges and break the cauliflower into florets. Cook both for 10 mins on one side and 5 mins on the other.

CRISPY *kale* SPOONS

Kale has been eaten for more than 2,000 years in different ways. Turn your leaves into spoons to scoop up the fresh and zesty guacamole.

Serves 4 · 5 mins · 5–8 mins

Tools

- Baking sheet or dish
- Oven mitts
- Spatula
- Sharp knife
- Cutting board
- Bowl
- Handheld blender

Ingredients

- 8 Tuscan kale leaves
- ¼ tsp salt

For the guacamole filling

- 1 avocado
- Juice of 1 lime
- 2 tbsp cilantro leaves
- ¼ tsp smoked paprika
- 2 green onions, finely sliced
- Freshly ground black pepper

1 Ask an adult to preheat the oven to 325°F (160°C). Place the kale leaves on the baking sheet or dish with the undersides up. Sprinkle with the salt. Bake for 4–5 mins, or until golden at the edges.

2 Then, carefully flip the kale leaves and bake them on the other side for 2–3 mins, or until crispy.

3 Ask an adult to peel and remove the pit from the avocado using the sharp knife on the cutting board.

4 In the bowl, blend all of the filling ingredients with the handheld blender. Dollop the filling onto the kale leaves and enjoy. The stems can be chewy, so discard them.

TOP TIP!

You can use your crispy kale spoons to season other dishes, by sprinkling the crispy bits on top of your meals.

For another topping, try the pesto from page 60.

Kale helps you stay healthy. It is packed with vitamins A, C, and calcium, so it's good for your eyes, hair, teeth, and nails.

Kale CRACKERS

These crackers have the perfect snap in your hands and crunch in your mouth. They're full of green goodness from the kale. They will keep fresh in an airtight container for up to 2 weeks.

 Makes 30   30 mins   10 mins

Tools

- Blender
- Sifter
- Large mixing bowl
- 3 baking sheets
- Parchment paper
- Rolling pin
- Blunt table knife
- Oven mitts

Ingredients

- 1 large Tuscan kale leaf or 2 small kale leaves, stems removed
- 8 sprigs of thyme, stems removed
- 5 giant goosefoot leaves (optional)
- 1 tsp agave or maple syrup
- 3½ cups whole-wheat spelt flour, chickpea flour, or buckwheat flour
- ½ tsp salt
- 1 tsp freshly cracked black pepper
- 1 tsp baking powder
- ¼ cup coconut oil, melted, or olive oil
- Basil pesto sauce, to serve (follow the cooking instructions on page 60)

(follow the cooking instructions on page 60)

 1 Put the kale, thyme leaves (not the stems), giant goosefoot (if using), agave or maple syrup, and ¼ cup of water into the blender. Blend until smooth.

 2 Sift the flour, salt, pepper, and baking powder into the bowl. After an adult has checked that the melted coconut oil has cooled, mix it in with your hands until the dough is crumbly.

3 Add ¼ cup of the kale smoothie and mix it in with your hands, until the dough comes together. If it's not binding, add more smoothie, or water, a teaspoon at a time, until it does. Do not overwork the dough.

 4 Ask an adult to preheat the oven to 350°F (180°C). Line each baking sheet with the parchment paper.

 5 Divide the dough into 3 balls and place 1 on each baking sheet. Then flatten the dough.

6 Place another sheet of parchment paper on top of the dough and, using the rolling pin, roll out the dough as thinly as possible.

7 Remove the top layer of parchment paper and ask an adult to carefully cut the dough into rectangles. Repeat with the other 2 balls of dough.

 8 Bake each sheet for 10 mins, or until the crackers are golden around the edges. Enjoy the crackers, warm or cold, with the basil pesto sauce.

•Level•
MEDIUM
•Rating•

TOP TIP!

The thinner you roll the dough, the better, as thin dough makes your crackers crunchier, and you get more crackers out of the dough.

Zucchini FRITTATA

A frittata is usually made with eggs, but this one is made with chickpea flour. Fill yours with delicious zucchini and dig in! Their mild, fresh taste makes zucchini the perfect pairing in this dish.

• Level •
MEDIUM
• Rating •

Serves 4   10 mins   18 mins

Tools

- Sharp knife
- Cutting board
- Grater
- Large mixing bowl
- Sifter
- Metal spoon
- Small mixing bowl
- Whisk
- 9-10in (22-24cm) cast-iron skillet
- Wooden spoon
- Ladle
- Oven mitts

Ingredients

- 1 medium-sized zucchini
- 1¼ cup chickpea flour
- 1 tsp ground turmeric
- ½ tsp baking powder
- 15-20 sprigs of thyme, stems removed and finely chopped
- 1 tbsp agave or maple syrup
- 1 tsp grated lemon zest
- Juice of 1 lemon
- Salt and freshly ground black pepper
- 1 tbsp olive oil
- 1 medium onion, finely sliced
- 3 garlic cloves, crushed
- Salad, to serve

⚠ 1 Ask an adult to preheat the broiler to high. Next, ask them to trim the ends off the zucchini and, using the large side of the grater, grate it coarsely.

2 In the large mixing bowl, sift together the chickpea flour, turmeric, and baking powder. Using the metal spoon, mix the ingredients until combined.

3 In the small mixing bowl, add the thyme, syrup, lemon zest and juice, salt and pepper, then stir in 1⅔ cup of water, a little at a time. Pour into the dry ingredients and whisk until combined into a thin, runny batter.

⚠ 4 Ask an adult to heat the oil in the skillet over medium-high heat. Carefully add the onion and garlic and sauté until lightly golden. Add the grated zucchini and cook for 2-3 mins. Keep stirring with the wooden spoon.

⚠ 5 Using the ladle, pour the batter evenly into the skillet and cook over medium heat for 2-3 mins, until the edges start to firm up. Do not stir the mixture.

⚠ 6 Ask an adult to put the pan under the broiler and cook for 3-5 mins, until the frittata has set and the top is golden. Remove and leave to cool slightly. Serve in slices with the salad.

TOP TIP!

If there is time, at step 3, set the fully combined batter aside for 1 hr. This makes it easier for you to digest the chickpeas.

⚠ Change IT UP!

There's always room to add another hero ingredient to this dish. At step 4, fry ½ cup coarsely grated butternut squash with the onion and garlic.

Zucchini give the bacteria in your gut what they love most: fiber! They are also full of potassium and vitamin C.

Zucchini LASAGNA

Have fun building this pasta-free lasagna by layering slices of zucchini, topping them with lentils and sauce, and repeating this step again and again.

Serves 6   25 mins   45-48 mins

Tools

- Sharp knife
- Cutting board
- Vegetable peeler
- Colander
- Bowl
- Paper towels
- Blender
- Large saucepan
- Wooden spoon
- Slotted spoon
- Medium saucepan
- Metal spoon
- 14in x 10in (35cm x 25cm) baking dish
- Oven mitts

YUM

For the lasagna

- 2 zucchini
- 1 tsp salt, plus extra for seasoning
- 1lb 8oz (725g) tomatoes
- 4 dates, pitted
- 1 tbsp olive oil
- 2 onions, diced
- 3 carrots, diced
- 11oz (325g) split red lentils, rinsed and drained
- 2 bay leaves
- 1 tsp freshly ground black pepper
- ¼ cup bread crumbs

For the white sauce

- 4 tbsp butter of your choice
- 1 leek, finely sliced
- ⅔ cup chickpea flour
- 2½ cups milk of your choice
- Grated zest and juice of 1 lemon
- 8 sprigs of fresh thyme, stems removed and chopped
- 1 tsp salt

 1 Ask an adult to carefully slice both ends off the zucchini, then hold each at an angle and drag the vegetable peeler lengthwise along the zucchini to make even slices. Stop when you get to the seeds.

2 Place the colander over the bowl. Add the zucchini slices and sprinkle with the salt. This will draw out some of their water. If the zucchini are still damp, pat them dry with the paper towels before using.

 3 Ask an adult to preheat the oven to 350°F (180°C) and blend the tomatoes and dates until smooth.

 4 Ask an adult to heat the oil in the large saucepan over medium heat. Add the onions and cook for 8-10 mins, or until softened and golden brown. Then add the carrots.

 5 Pour the blended mixture into the saucepan and, using the wooden spoon, stir in the lentils, bay leaves, and 1 cup of water. Season with salt and pepper.

6 Carefully bring to a boil and simmer for 15 mins, until the mixture has thickened and the lentils are soft. Set aside and use the slotted spoon to carefully remove the bay leaves.

7 To make the white sauce, ask an adult to melt the butter in the medium saucepan over low heat. Add the sliced leek and cook for 2-3 mins, until softened. Stir in the chickpea flour, then add the milk, a little at a time, stirring until the mixture is smooth and creamy. Stir in the lemon zest and juice, thyme, and salt. If time, let rest for 1 hr.

8 Now the building begins! Start with a layer of lentil mix at the bottom of the baking dish. This will keep the lasagna from sticking. Now add a layer of zucchini slices, cover with a layer of lentil mix, then spread on the white sauce. Repeat this process twice, for 10 layers altogether.

9 Sprinkle the bread crumbs over your final layer of white sauce. Cook in the oven for 20 mins, or until golden and bubbling.

Squash MUFFINS

Thanks to the grated butternut squash, these muffins are moist, with a sweet, nutty flavor. With raspberries baked on top, they look amazing, and taste even better.

• Level •
EASY
• Rating •

Makes 18   20 mins   25–30 mins

Tools

• 18 paper cupcake cases
• 2 x 12-hole cupcake pans
• Sharp knife
• Cutting board
• Metal spoon
• Vegetable peeler
• Grater
• Large mixing bowl
• Fork
• Electric mixer
• Sifter
• Oven mitts
• Wire rack

Ingredients

• Extra virgin olive oil, for greasing
• 4oz (115g) butternut squash
• 3½oz (100g) banana (1 banana)
• 6 tbsp flax "egg"
• ½ cup agave or maple syrup
• 4 tbsp coconut oil, melted
• ½ cup apple sauce
• 1½ tsp cinnamon
• 1 tbsp pure vanilla extract
• ¼ tsp salt
• 1 tsp baking soda
• ½ tsp baking powder
• ½ cup milk of your choice
• ¾ cup oats
• ⅔ cup chickpea flour
• 1 cup + 4 tbsp buckwheat flour
• 54 raspberries

 1 Ask an adult to preheat the oven to 375°F (190°C). Place the 18 paper cases in the cupcake pans. Most pans have 12 holes, so you need to use 2 pans. Lightly grease the cases.

 2 Ask an adult to prepare the butternut squash by using the sharp knife to cut the squash in half lengthwise. Scoop out the seeds with the metal spoon and remove the skin using the peeler. Carefully cut the squash into big chunks. Using the large side of the grater, coarsely grate each chunk.

 3 In the large mixing bowl, mash the banana with the fork. Using the electric mixer and in the same bowl, ask an adult to beat together the mashed banana, flax "egg," agave or maple syrup, and melted coconut oil until they form a smooth, runny batter.

Squash comes in all different shapes, colors, and sizes. Did you know that pumpkins are a type of squash that has been grown for more than 10,000 years?

Remember that flax "egg" is 3 tbsp flax seeds and 3 tbsp water stirred together. It then is allowed to rest for 10 mins.

4 Add the apple sauce, cinnamon, vanilla extract, salt, baking soda, baking powder, and milk. Beat together until thick and well mixed. Then stir in the grated butternut squash and oats.

 5 Sift the chickpea flour and buckwheat flour over the top, add in any grains left in the sifter, and whisk to form a light-brown mixture. If you have time, set the mixture aside for 1 hr. Spoon into the paper cases and top each muffin with 3 raspberries.

 6 Bake for 25-30 mins, until risen and golden brown. Swap the cupcake pans around halfway through baking. Once baked, ask an adult to place the pans on the wire rack to cool completely.

FUN FACT!

The name "squash" comes from the Narragansett Native American word "askutasquash," which means "eaten raw or uncooked." You can eat squash raw or cooked, in salads, cakes, stews, and pies.

Corn SOUP

Corn, pumpkins, and peas grow well together. Our hero ingredient and its sidekicks also taste great together in this chunky soup.

• Level •
MEDIUM
• Rating •

Serves 6   20 mins   35–40 mins

Tools

- Cutting board
- Sharp knife
- Strainer
- Blender
- Large saucepan with lid
- Wooden spoon
- 6 soup bowls

Ingredients

- 4 fresh corncobs
- 5½oz (150g) dried yellow split peas
- 1 large onion, coarsely sliced
- 6–8 garlic cloves
- 2 celery ribs, coarsely sliced
- 2 tbsp thyme, stems removed
- 2 tbsp cilantro leaves
- 2 tbsp coconut oil
- 1 tbsp ground cumin
- ¼ tsp ground cloves
- 1lb 2oz (500g) pumpkin, or butternut squash, carefully peeled, seeded, and cut into small cubes
- 4 carrots, sliced
- 1 vegetable bouillon cube, dissolved in 4½ cups of boiling water
- 1¾ cups coconut milk

1 Ask an adult to carefully cut each cob into equal quarters. Place each cob flat on the cutting board and, moving the sharp knife in a rocking motion, slice downward to cut the quarters.

2 Put the split peas in the stainer and rinse them under cold water until the water runs clear. Set aside. Ask an adult to blend the onion, garlic, celery, thyme, and cilantro in the blender until a thick paste forms.

3 Ask an adult to carefully melt the coconut oil in the pan over medium heat. Pour in the blended mixture, along with the cumin and cloves, and sauté for 2–5 mins.

4 Ask an adult to add the split peas to the saucepan with the corncobs, pumpkin or squash, and carrots. Cook for 2–3 mins, until the vegetables have softened.

5 Carefully pour in the bouillon and coconut milk, so the liquid covers the vegetables. Bring to a boil, then cover and simmer for 30 mins, or until the split peas are soft. Stir occasionally. Serve in the soup bowls.

TOP TIP!

Any leftover soup can be stored in an airtight container and frozen for up to 3 months.

Level
EASY
Rating

ROASTED corn RIBS

Juicy on the inside, with a smoky coating, these corn ribs are perfect for eating with your hands. Eat the corn kernels, then compost the rest when you're done!

Makes 8   10 mins   30 mins

Tools

- Sharp knife
- Cutting board
- Baking dish
- Small bowl
- Metal spoon
- Oven mitts

Ingredients

- 2 fresh corncobs, soaked in water for 15–30 mins
- 3 tbsp butter of your choice
- 1 garlic clove, crushed
- 3 bay leaves
- 10 sprigs of thyme, stems removed, plus extra to garnish
- 1 tsp salt
- 1 tsp smoked paprika

1 Preheat your oven to 350°F (180°C). Ask an adult to cut each corncob lengthwise into 4 pieces. Hold the cobs upright and, moving the sharp knife in a rocking motion, carefully slice downward through the center. Repeat with each half and place in the baking dish.

2 In the small bowl, mix the butter, garlic, bay leaves, thyme, salt, and smoked paprika. Use the metal spoon to coat each piece of corn in the mixture.

3 Ask an adult to place the dish in the preheated oven. Bake for 30 mins, or until the corn is golden brown. Halfway through baking, ask an adult to carefully spoon the melted mixture in the baking dish over the corn.

4 Leave the cooked corn until it is cool enough to handle. Before serving, remove the bay leaves, then garnish with the extra thyme.

Magic CHICKPEA HUMMUS

Turn your chickpeas into a dip and dunk any of our hero ingredients in it.

• Level •
EASY
• Rating •

TOP TIP!

You must soak uncooked chickpeas and borlotti beans in water for 24 hrs before you use them.

Serves 10   5 mins   5-8 mins

Tools

- Large saucepan
- Colander
- Small skillet
- Blender
- Large serving bowl

Ingredients

- 5oz (140g) sprouted chickpeas; if you haven't sprouted the chickpeas, use canned chickpeas, drained and rinsed
- 4 garlic cloves
- 1½ tsp dried cumin
- 4 dates, pitted
- ½ cup tahini
- ⅓ cup olive oil
- 2 tbsp cold water
- 2 tsp dried rosemary
- 1 tsp salt
- Sprinkle of freshly ground black pepper
- Juice of 2 lemons
- Thinly sliced vegetables, such as bell peppers, cucumbers, and radishes, or chips, to serve

⚠ 1 If using sprouted chickpeas, ask an adult to boil water in the large saucepan. Carefully add the chickpeas, leave to boil for 2-3 mins, then drain in the colander.

⚠ 2 In the skillet, carefully roast the garlic over medium heat for 3-5 mins, stirring frequently. Then add the cumin and roast until the spice's scent is released and the garlic is soft.

⚠ 3 Set a handful of chickpeas aside. Whiz all the ingredients in the blender until smooth. If the mixture is too thick or dry, add more water, oil, or lemon juice, a tablespoon at a time, until the desired texture is achieved.

4 Transfer the dip into the large serving bowl, garnish with the remaining chickpeas, and serve with vegetables or chips. It's also great as a sandwich filler.

Leftover hummus can be stored in the fridge in a container, covered with olive oil, for up to 1 week.

You can also serve the sauce in a tortilla wrap with some avocado, crispy lettuce, and rice.

Mexican mole BEANS

Chocolate adds richness to this delicious bean recipe, without making it sweet. Packed with protein, the beans in this dish work hard behind the scenes to keep your body working properly.

Serves 8   15 mins   60 mins

•Level•
MEDIUM
•Rating•

Tools

- Large saucepan with lid
- Colander
- Blender
- Wooden spoon
- Metal spoon

Ingredients

- 14oz (400g) borlotti or cranberry beans; if you haven't grown the beans, use canned beans, drained and rinsed
- 2 large dates, pitted
- 8 sun-dried tomatoes, in oil, drained
- 1lb 5oz (600g) tomatoes
- 1 large onion, finely diced
- 1 celery rib, finely diced
- 4 garlic cloves, crushed
- 2 tbsp coconut oil, melted
- 1 tbsp smoked paprika
- 4 tsp ground cumin
- 1 tsp ground allspice
- ¼ tsp ground cloves
- 10 sprigs of thyme, stems removed
- 1 cinnamon stick
- 1 vegetable bouillon cube
- 2 tbsp smooth peanut butter or tahini
- 1½oz (45g) dark chocolate (72%)
- 1 tsp salt
- Juice of 1 lime
- Toast, to serve
- 2 avocados, pitted and sliced, to serve
- Grated lime zest, to serve

1 If using fresh borlotti beans, ask an adult to boil them in the saucepan for 30-40 mins, then drain in the colander. Set aside. Blend together the dates, sun-dried tomatoes, and tomatoes until smooth.

2 In the same saucepan, sauté the onion, celery, and garlic in the melted coconut oil over medium heat for 2 mins. Stir in the herbs and spices.

3 Carefully add the blended mixture, bouillon cube, peanut butter or tahini, and ⅓ cup of water to the pan. Simmer for 10 mins. The sauce should be thick and smell delicious.

4 Add the chocolate. Once melted, add the beans and salt, cover, and simmer for 10 mins on medium heat, until the beans are tender. Add more water if the sauce is too thick.

5 Use the metal spoon to carefully remove the cinnamon stick, then stir in the lime juice. Serve on toast with the sliced avocado and top with the lime zest.

TOP TIP!

Press the bay leaf into the excess pastry you've trimmed off. Carefully cut around the leaf shape. Make more than 1 if you have enough pastry.

Spinach AND leek TART

This tart is full of iron-rich spinach and has a sweet flavor. Iron in your food is like a superhero that keeps your body strong and healthy.

Serves 6-8   20 mins   50 mins

• Level •
MEDIUM
• Rating •

Tools

- 9in x 9in (23cm x 23cm) baking dish
- Large mixing bowl
- 2 forks
- Metal spoon
- Frying pan
- Sharp knife
- Parchment paper
- Baking beans
- Oven mitts
- Foil

Ingredients

- 1 tsp olive oil, for greasing
- 1¼ cup milk of your choice
- ⅔ cup chickpea flour
- ¼ cup buckwheat flour
- ¼ tsp nutmeg, ground or grated
- ½ tsp dried tarragon
- 5-7 sprigs of thyme, stems removed (optional)
- ½ tsp salt
- Freshly ground black pepper
- 1 low-salt vegetable bouillon cube
- 1 small leek, finely sliced
- 2 tbsp butter of your choice
- 3⅓ cups spinach leaves
- 11oz (320g) puff pastry, premade
- Bay leaf, to make a pastry garnish (see TIP! on page 82)
- 12 cherry tomatoes and 3 medium-sized tomatoes, sliced, to serve

1 Ask an adult to preheat the oven to 400°F (200°C). Grease the baking dish with the olive oil.

2 In the large mixing bowl, use a fork to combine the milk, both types of flour, nutmeg, tarragon, thyme (if using), salt, and pepper.

3 When the filling is smooth and thick enough to coat the back of the spoon, crumble in the bouillon cube. If time, let the filling rest for 1 hr. In the frying pan, sauté the leek in the butter until softened. Remove from the heat; add the spinach, then mix in with the filling.

4 Place the puff pastry in the baking dish. Ask an adult to use the knife to trim excess dough off the edge. Prick the bottom of the crust all over with a fork. Place a piece of parchment paper on the bottom.

5 Pour the baking beans on the parchment paper. Ask an adult to blind-bake the crust in the oven for 15 mins, then remove the parchment and beans. Be careful—they'll be hot.

6 Pour the filling into the crust. Lay the pastry leaf shapes on top, then cover with the foil. Ask an adult to bake for 25-30 mins, until the filling is just set. Uncover for 5 mins to brown. Serve with slices of tomato.

Enjoy this dish with a glass of orange juice—with the pulp in, as pulp adds more fiber. Vitamin C from the oranges helps your body to absorb the iron from the spinach.

 Makes ¼ cup

 5 mins

 5 mins

PUFFED *amaranth*

Corn isn't the only grain that can be popped. You can puff (pop) amaranth, too! The seeds have a nutty flavor. If you puff them, you can add them to granola or use them to make tasty cookies.

⚠️1 Ask an adult to heat the saucepan over high heat for 5 mins, until very hot. Carefully add the amaranth, spreading it out to cover the bottom of the pan, then step back, as the amaranth should begin popping almost instantly.

Tools

- Large, deep saucepan
- Wooden spoon
- Glass jar

Ingredients

- 1 tbsp amaranth grain

⚠️2 Ask an adult to keep stirring the amaranth with the spoon to ensure the grains pop evenly and none burn—this is the tricky bit. Don't cover the pan, because you want the steam to escape.

⚠️3 Once amaranth's delicious nutty smell is released and you can see more white puffed amaranth than brown seeds, ask an adult to take the pan off the heat.

POP

4 Let the puffed amaranth cool completely, then add it to your granola or cookie mix. Store it in the glass jar if you don't want to use it immediately.

• Level •
MEDIUM
• Rating •

FUN FACT!

Amaranth is small, but very mighty. It's packed with nutrients that your body needs to stay strong and healthy, including protein, fiber, iron, and calcium.

Amaranth has been grown for thousands of years. It was an important food for the Aztecs, who lived in Mexico from the 1300s to the 1500s.

84

Amaranth GRANOLA

Start your day off with this delicious granola. It'll make you and your taste buds feel good.

 Serves 4

 20 mins

20-25 mins

Tools

- 16in x 10½in (40cm x 26cm) baking dish
- Parchment paper
- Small heatproof bowl
- Large mixing bowl
- Wooden spoon
- Oven mitts

Ingredients

- 5 tbsp puffed amaranth grain
- 4 tbsp coconut oil
- 2 cups old-fashioned oats
- ¼ cup sunflower seeds
- ½ cup pumpkin seeds (or use any seeds that you enjoy)
- ¼ cup hazelnuts (optional)
- 1 tsp cinnamon
- 4 tbsp agave or maple syrup
- ½ tsp salt
- ½ cup dried mulberries or goji berries (optional)

1 Ask an adult to preheat the oven to 350°F (180°C). Line the baking dish with parchment paper. Follow the recipe on page 84 to puff the amaranth.

2 Ask an adult to melt the coconut oil in the microwave in the heatproof bowl. It should take about 1 min.

3 In the large mixing bowl, combine the puffed amaranth, oats, sunflower and pumpkin seeds, hazelnuts (if using), cinnamon, agave or maple syrup, salt, and melted coconut oil. Gently stir with the wooden spoon until evenly mixed.

4 Pour the mixture into the baking dish and spread it out evenly. Bake for 20-25 mins, mixing it every 8 mins, until the granola becomes crispy.

5 Remove from the oven and let the granola cool for 30 mins. Then add the mulberries or goji berries (if using) or a dried fruit of your choice.

•Level• **MEDIUM** •Rating•

YUM!!

Amaranth seeds can be cooked and eaten like a grain or popped like popcorn or saved and used to grow more plants!

DELISH!

Enjoy with a glass of milk of your choice.

Amaranth
CHOC CHIP COOKIES

Who doesn't enjoy sweet and chewy chocolate chip cookies? Adding amaranth supercharges your cookies with lots of things your body loves.

• Level •
MEDIUM
• Rating •

Makes 15

20 mins, plus 30 mins chilling

16-20 mins

Tools

- 2 baking sheets
- Parchment paper
- Large mixing bowl
- Electric mixer
- Metal spoon
- Tablespoon
- Oven mitts
- Wire rack
- Spatula

Ingredients

- 1 tbsp flax "egg"
- 3 tbsp butter of your choice, softened
- ¼ cup coconut oil
- 1 cup sugar (we like to use coconut sugar)
- 1 tbsp pure vanilla extract
- ¼ cup puffed amaranth grain
- ½ cup spelt flour
- ½ cup white flour
- ¼ cup buckwheat flour
- ½ tsp baking soda
- ½ tsp baking powder
- ½ tsp salt
- ¾ cup chocolate chips

1 Line 2 baking sheets with parchment paper to stop the cookies from sticking as they bake. Then turn to page 56 for how to make flax "egg."

2 In the large mixing bowl, beat together the butter, coconut oil, and sugar with the electric mixer for 3-4 mins, until pale and fluffy. Beat in the flax "egg" and vanilla extract. Then follow the recipe on page 84 to puff the amaranth.

3 Add each type of flour, baking soda, baking powder, and salt to the mixture, and mix together until everything combines to form a stiff dough. Using the metal spoon, stir in the chocolate chips and puffed amaranth. Place in the fridge to chill for 30 mins.

4 Ask an adult to preheat the oven to 375°F (190°C). Roll the dough into 15 balls and place on the parchment paper, leaving a space around each ball so that they can spread as they bake. Flatten them slightly with the back of the tablespoon.

5 Ask an adult to place the baking sheets in the oven. Bake for 16-20 mins, or until golden. Remove the baking sheets from the oven and leave the cookies to set for 5 mins, before placing them on the wire rack using the spatula.

Change IT UP!

At step 3, replace half the chocolate chips with an equal amount of dried goji berries to give your cookies a boost of vitamins A and C.

Berry COBBLER

Fluffy on the outside, with a tangy raspberry filling, every slice of this dessert is bursting with flavor.

• Level •
TRICKY
• Rating •

Serves 8 | 15 mins | 40–45 mins

Tools

- 14in x 10in (35cm x 25cm) baking dish
- Wooden spoon
- Small saucepan
- Large mixing bowl
- Spatula
- Metal spoon
- Oven mitts
- Wire rack

Ingredients

- 1lb 8oz (700g) raspberries
- 1 tbsp all-purpose flour
- Grated zest of ½ lemon
- 1 tsp vanilla extract
- 1 tbsp agave or maple syrup
- ¼ tsp ground cardamom (optional)
- Coconut yogurt, to serve

For the batter

- 1 tbsp coconut oil
- 1 cup white spelt flour
- 1 cup buckwheat flour
- 1 tbsp flax seeds
- ½ tsp baking powder
- 2 cups milk of your choice
- ½ cup agave or maple syrup

1 Ask an adult to preheat the oven to 375°F (190°C). In the baking dish, use the wooden spoon to gently mix together the raspberries, all-purpose flour, lemon zest, vanilla, agave or maple syrup, and cardamom (if using). Be careful not to crush the berries.

2 Ask an adult to melt the coconut oil in the small saucepan over low heat. In the large mixing bowl, mix the dry ingredients for the batter with the spatula.

3 Add the milk, melted coconut oil, and agave or maple syrup, and stir well until the mixture is smooth and thick enough to coat the back of the metal spoon.

4 Pour the batter over the berry mixture in the baking dish. Ask an adult to place the cobbler in the oven and bake for 40–45 mins, until risen. If the top starts to get too dark, cover it with foil for the last 5 mins.

5 Ask an adult to take the cobbler out of the oven. Leave it to cool on the wire rack, then serve with a dollop of coconut yogurt.

Change IT UP!

You can make the filling of this dessert with other types of fruit.

For a mixed berry cobbler, use 9oz (250g) of raspberries, 9oz (250g) of blackberries, and 7oz (200g) of blueberries.

In fall or winter, swap raspberries for the same quantity of peeled and chopped apples or pears.

TOP TIP!

Freeze a batch of your homegrown raspberries, so you always have some on hand. This means you'll have berry cobbler, as well as a boost of vitamin C, all year round.

Food WASTE

You can do your bit to look after the environment, even if it's just planting one seed on your windowsill. One clever way to be a guardian of the Earth is by reducing your food waste.

THE PROBLEM OF WASTE

Nearly a third of all food is wasted each year, and most of the waste happens at home. When food is wasted, the energy and water it took to make it is also wasted. If the food goes to garbage sites called landfills, it produces a gas that warms up the Earth.

Make your food go further

Whether you have leftovers or you want to keep ingredients fresh for longer, storing your food properly is a great way of reducing food waste. Put fruits and veggies such as berries, leafy greens, and carrots in the fridge, use airtight containers for snacks or sauces, and freeze leftovers in small portions. Make sure to check the use-by date on all ingredients.

Food can last longer in the freezer.

Ripe, not rotten

Sometimes fruits such as avocados or plums aren't ripe and ready to eat when you buy them, so you might miss the chance to enjoy them before they go bad. A clever way to prevent food waste is to place unripe fruits next to bananas. Bananas release a gas that speeds up the ripening process.

You can leave potato skins on.

Use carrot peelings in stocks or soups.

Oranges are a treat for your body and your home.

Super scraps

A lot of the food that is thrown away can be used. Some vegetable peelings can be baked in the oven until crispy and used as crunchy snacks or salad decorations. You can even put dried orange peel in a bowl to make your home smell fresh.

Cupboard challenge

It's good to clear out your cupboards (and fridge) regularly to make sure you use up food before it spoils. What can you make from your supplies? Mix up old recipes with new ingredients, or create a platter of different snacks. Use your imagination and get creative!

Look through our recipes to see how you can repurpose leftover ingredients.

Transform waste into soil magic

Anything you can't use up, you can compost (except for meat, dairy, and oily foods). Mixing your waste veggies and fruits with dried leaves and grass clippings can create a powerful compost for your plants. It's the circle of life, from soil to soil, with no waste!

GLOSSARY

ABSORB
To take in or soak up something

AMINO ACID
An organic molecule that makes up proteins

ANTIOXIDANT
A substance found in some foods that helps the body fight against the damaging effects of free radicals

APHID
A small insect that sucks sap from plants

BACTERIA
The most common group of microbes, which are found everywhere, including in the body. Some are dangerous and may cause disease, and others are beneficial

BEST-BEFORE DATE
A guideline date of when a food's quality may start to decrease. This doesn't refer to food's safety, so food past this date is often fine to eat

BUG
A small insect or other small creature

BULB
An underground part of a plant that can be planted to grow into a full plant. Onions are bulbs

CANE
The stem of a plant

CARBON DIOXIDE
A colorless gas that is found in the air

CAROTENOID
Yellow, red, and orange pigments found in some plants, fruits, and vegetables, which give them their color

CHAFF
The outer part or casing of a grain, such as wheat, that is removed before it is used

CLAY SOIL
Tiny pieces of ground-up rock that stick together

COMPANION PLANTING
Planting plants that can help each other grow and protect each other from pests close together

COMPOST
A mixture of vegetable waste and rotten plants that is added to the soil

CROP
Plants that are grown in large amounts and used for food

CUT-AND-COME-AGAIN
A plant that is repeatedly cut or harvested in order to keep the plant growing

DIGESTION
The process of breaking down food into smaller molecules called nutrients, which your body can use

DRAINAGE
The process by which water moves across and out of the soil or compost

EDIBLE
Something that is safe to eat and is not poisonous

EGG
The female reproductive part of a plant

ENZYME
A substance that speeds up chemical reactions, such as breaking down food for digestion and growing new cells

FERTILIZER
A substance that helps plants to grow

FLOWER
The part of a plant where the male and female parts are found

FREE RADICAL
A particle that is unstable because it doesn't have all of the pieces it needs. It can attach to human cells and cause damage to the body

FROST
Ice that forms when water freezes

FRUIT
The part of a plant that forms when a flower is pollinated

FUNGI
A life-form that feeds on rotting or dead things. Mold and mushrooms are fungi

HARVEST
Cutting and collecting plants when they are ready to be picked

HEIRLOOM
Something passed down from one generation to the next

INSECT
A small animal with no backbone, six legs, and generally one or two pairs of wings

LOAM SOIL
A mixture of sand, silt, and clay soil. This is a type of soil that is good for growing most plants

MANURE
Animal poop used to make soil richer and full of nutrients

MICROBE
Tiny living creature that can only be seen through a microscope, also known as a microorganism. Bacteria, viruses, and mold are all examples of microbes

MICROSCOPIC
Things that are so small they can only be seen with a microscope

MINERAL
A naturally occurring solid made of crystals

MULCH
A layer covering the surface of the soil that keeps in moisture

NECTAR
The sweet liquid made by the flower of a plant

NITROGEN
A colorless gas that makes up most of the atmosphere

NUTRIENT
Food used by living things so they can survive and grow

OMEGAS
Healthy fatty acids, such as Omega-3, that are found in some foods

ORGANISM
Any living thing, such as animals and plants

OXYGEN
A colorless gas in the air

PEST
An insect or other animal that attack plants

PESTICIDE
A substance used for getting rid of insects or other organisms that harm plants

pH
A figure that shows how acidic or alkaline a liquid is

PHOTOSYNTHESIS
A process by which plants make their own food using the energy from sunlight

PLUMP
When something has a full and round shape

POLLEN
A fine powder, usually yellow or orange, that is needed for plants to produce more seeds

POLLINATION
When pollen is moved from one flower to another to make more of the same flower

POLLINATOR
An animal, such as a bee or butterfly, that carries pollen from one flower to another

PREDATOR
An animal that eats another animal

RECYCLE
Finding a new use for something you have used, either yourself, or by putting it into a recycling bin

REDUCE
To cut down or make smaller

REFINED SUGAR
Sugar that has been produced or processed from naturally occurring sources

REUSE
Use again, instead of throwing something away

RIPE
Something that is ready to pick and eat

ROTTED
Something that has gone bad

SAND SOIL
Soil that has large particles and is like the sand you would find on the beach

SEED
A case that contains everything needed to grow a new plant

SEEDLING
A young plant that has grown from a seed

SHOOT
New growth in plants that leads to leaves and flowers developing

SIDE SHOOT
A shoot growing from the side of a plant's stem

SILT SOIL
Soil with medium-sized particles made from rock and minerals

SMOKE POINT
The temperature at which oil starts to smoke

SOW
To plant a seed on or in the soil

SPROUT
A seed that has just begun to grow

STEM
The main stalk of a plant

TAPROOT
A root that grows downward into the soil. Carrots are taproots

THINNING
Moving plants farther apart or removing parts of a plant to make more space for the plants to grow

TRUE LEAVES
The second set of leaves to grow that provide fuel and energy to plants via photosynthesis

USE-BY DATE
The date a food should be eaten by, before it starts to go bad

VARIETIES
Different forms or types of the same category

WASTE
All the things we throw away

WEEDS
Wild plants that grow in areas they are not wanted and that prevent the plants that are wanted from growing properly

INDEX

ACKNOWLEDGMENTS

DK would like to thank the following people for their assistance in the preparation of this book: Anne Damerell for legal assistance, Anna Bonnerjea for design assistance, Sophie Parkes for editorial assistance, Charlotte Simpkins for testing the Spinach and leek tart recipe, Sarah Bailey for photographic assistance, Caroline Stamps for proofreading, and Helen Peters for compiling the index.

The publisher would like to thank the following for their kind permission to reproduce their photographs:

(Key: a-above; b-below/bottom; c-center; f-far; l-left; r-right; t-top)

6 Dreamstime.com: Deyangeorgiev (bc). 8 Dorling Kindersley: Barnabas Kindersley (br). Dreamstime.com: Katerina Kovaleva / Kkovaleva (tl). 9 Dreamstime.com: Irochka (tr). 11 Science Photo Library: Bo Veisland, Mi&l (bl). 12 Dorling Kindersley: Barnabas Kindersley (br). Dreamstime.com: Kenmind76 (crb/Pear); Katerina Kovaleva / Kkovaleva (crb/Watermelon); Pipa100 (crb/Orange). 15 Dreamstime.com: Draftmode (cra/Butternut squash). 16 Dreamstime.com: Draftmode (cr/Butternut squash); Sally Scott (ca/Rhubarb). Getty Images: felipedupouy.com / Photodisc (cra/carrots). 17 123RF.com: Karandaev (crb/Coconut); olegdudko (cla/Kiwi); Suradech Kongkiatpaiboon (cra/Millet). Dreamstime.com: Kateryna Bibro (ca/Vitelotte potato); Boonchuay Iamsumang (clb/Cucumber); Anton Ignatenco (cra/Almonds). Getty Images: Foodcollection / Image Professionals GmbH (ca/blackberries). 18-19 Dreamstime.com: Irochka (ca). 19 123RF.com: Duncan Noakes (bc). 21 Dreamstime.com: Tamara Kulikova (cra/Soil); Anton Starikov (cra/compost); Chee Siong Teh / Tehcheesiong (c). 22 Dreamstime.com: Alena Brozova (cra); Ingrid Heczko (br). Getty Images / iStock: visual7 (crb). 26 Dreamstime.com: Darren Curzon (tc); Roman Milert (bc). Getty Images / iStock: Mukhina1 (tr). 27 Dreamstime.com: Joseph Gough (bl); Karin Hildebrand Lau (tc); Hanmon (tr); Winai Tepsuttinun (cra); Hilda Weges (crb); (bc). 28 Dreamstime.com: Thomaspicture (c). 29 Alamy Stock Photo: Rosemary Calvert (cra/lavender). Dreamstime.com: Marina Lohrbach (cra); Alfio Scisetti (cra/Sunflower). 31 Dreamstime.com: Stephan Bock (crb/potatoes); Picture Partners (tr); HongChan001 (br). 33 Dreamstime.com: Crystal Taylor (cl); Birute Vijeikiene (cr). 34 123RF.com: Mariusz Blach (c/Cup). Dreamstime.com: Airborne77 (cb); Amnachphoto (cl); Aperturesound (c/Shoe); Anton Starikov (cr). 36 Dreamstime.com: Pstedrak (cra/Thyme). 38 123RF.com: Jean-Paul Chassenet (bl). 39 Dreamstime.com: Alexander Raths (r). 40 Depositphotos Inc: griffin024 (tr). 41 Dreamstime.com: Anna Kucherova (tc); Natika (tr); Nevinates (cra). 43 Dreamstime.com: Photographyfirm (l).

44 Dreamstime.com: Alfio Scisetti (tr). 45 Alamy Stock Photo: Chesh (tr). Shutterstock.com: BriXio (br). 46 Dreamstime.com: Horst Lieber (cra). 47 Dreamstime.com: Brenda Carson (tr); Karsten Eggert (r); Sarah Marchant (tc). 48 Dreamstime.com: Antonio Scarpi (bc). 50 Dreamstime.com: Marilyn Barbone (bc). 51 Dreamstime.com: Esben Hansen (bc); Quanthem (bc/Kale). 53 Alamy Stock Photo: blickwinkel / McPHOTO / HRM (r). Dreamstime.com: Lepas (tc, tr); Valentyn75 (cra). 55 Dreamstime. com: Stuartbur (ca/Knife). 58 Dreamstime.com: Chernetskaya (cr/Chickpea flour , cr); Milart1964 (c); Rafael Angel Irusta Machin (bl/Oil); Gita Kulinica (bc/Pasta); Elena Schweitzer (br). 59 Dreamstime.com: Barbro Bergfeldt (crb/Vanilla); Birgit Reitz Hofmann (crb/Pine nut); Marian Vejcik (tr); Chernetskaya (cla, clb/Coriander); Oksana Ermak (ca); Elizabeth Cummings (ca/Sugar); Lim Seng Kui (cra/crb); ItalianFoodPro (crb/Artichoke); Difenbahia (bl/Tarragon); Mohamed Osama (bc/Cardamom); Sergey Kolesnikov (bc). 73 Dreamstime.com: Draftmode (cla). 76 Dreamstime.com: Draftmode (tl). 81 Dreamstime.com: Antonio Scarpi (tl). 84 Depositphotos Inc: spline_x (tl). 87 Depositphotos Inc: spline_x (tl). 88 Dreamstime.com: Alessio Cola / Alexpacha (cra); Yvdavyd (cra/Blackberries); GCapture (crb/Pear). 90 Dreamstime.com: Chernetskaya (cb). 91 Alamy Stock Photo: Hugh Threlfall (tl). Dreamstime.com: Igor Zakharevich (cla). Getty Images: felipedupouy.com / Photodisc (cla/Carrots)

All other images © Dorling Kindersley